Innocent Nightmare

My Journey, My Perspective

By
Roosevelt Glenn

This book is dedicated to those who always believed in me and never doubted me.

And ye **shall** *know* **the truth,** *and* **the truth
shall** *make* **you free.**
John 8:32 NIV

<u>Introduction</u>

The following pages recount the life and times of Roosevelt Glenn, a man imprisoned for a crime he did not commit. As I helped him tell his story, I was often struck by the character of this man. Yes, the character of a man found guilty of an awful crime.

Crime and character are partners in this story as they both affect the core of the man. But one is the man and one is not. For he could not have had the strength of character that he possesses and have committed the crime for which he was imprisoned.

In telling his story, I was reminded of the story of Joseph in the Bible. In the midst of facing horrible things, Joseph's character and integrity were pushed to the surface. Joseph simply did not allow external circumstances to change who he decided he was created to be. Like Joseph, Roosevelt had to make decisions to be the man he was created to be rather than man his circumstances, the justice system and his environment tried to say he was.

There are not many of us who would stay true to

ourselves after years of being told something different, years of living a life that was contrary to what we thought, years of being shut down and shut out.

It might not seem worth the fight to try to convince everyone, anyone or even ourselves that we were not "that". Whatever "that" was at the time - bad, wrong, stupid, worthless, unloved, evil, ugly, liar or failure.

Everyone faces times when it doesn't seem worth the fight. In the end, we hear it, then we think it, then we believe it and finally we become it.

But it doesn't have to be that way.

Joseph heard it, experienced it and yet he stayed true to the goodness in his nature and in the end he won.

Roosevelt Glenn heard it every time the gavel dropped, he experienced it for nearly 17 years in prison for a crime he did not commit and through it all he stayed true to the goodness in his nature.

Each chapter of his journey reminds me to think about who I have chosen to be and to examine how much power I have given over to circumstances and other people to affect my decision.

For as I think, so I am (Proverbs 23:7). Roosevelt's journey encouraged me to value who I was created to be enough to stick to it. Not in the self-centered, narcissistic way our society teaches but to be willing to stand up for and sometimes fight for myself in spite of my environment, my mistakes or even the choices of those around me.

So many of us would make the "loss" of time, family, life, money and the unfairness of the situation to be the defining moment in our lives. And we might be justified in doing so. This story publicly acknowledges the travesty of justice that has played out in the life of this man.

But what it also acknowledges is that the true defining moment wasn't his imprisonment. Roosevelt's defining moment was when he decided to stay true to himself and God rather than fall prey to what the victim, the legal system, the media, the public and the environment said about him.

It was in that moment, Roosevelt Glenn won.

~ Cheryl Conway Griffith

*So if the Son **sets you free**,*
*you will be **free indeed**.*
John 8:36 NIV

The Release

Suddenly, I could breathe.

Well, it wasn't really suddenly but I did feel a release. As if I'd been holding my breath ... for over 16 years.

My body was trembling and my mind was simply trying to grasp what was happening to me much like in the beginning. It felt unreal but this time it was more like a dream than a nightmare. I had waited over 16 years to hear the officer tell me to pack and inventory my property because I was being released from prison in the morning.

It didn't take long for me to pack. I'd gotten rid of everything except the essentials because there was nothing, I mean nothing, that was worth taking home as a memento. This wasn't some wonderful vacation; it was my nightmare coming to an end. There were no fond memories and I just wanted to forget as much as possible about this lifetime, this incarceration.

I followed instructions, I packed and went to bed on my bunk for the last night. I slept the sleep of a free man and woke refreshed with adrenaline pumping even as I went through the normal routine of showering and shaving.

It was a new day in every sense of the word, this is the day I would be who I should have always been, who I always was ... a free and innocent man.

There was a catch in my throat as I tried to tell the guard I was ready. I grabbed my belongings and shouted "Hallelujah, I'm out of here" as I left my cell for the last time. Not for breakfast or work detail but to regain my life.

I was surprised to see inmates, convicts and staff members waiting to say goodbye. With handshakes and well wishes, prayers and encouragement to be strong, not come back and even some who hated to see me go but knew that it was the right thing.

Signing my release papers stole my breath for a moment. It felt like it was over but I still had to leave, I had to get out of the facility. Thankfully, there were no surprises, no delays, nothing tripping me up. I rode in a van to the warehouse area. The air was crisp, somehow fresher. Leaves were bursting with color. I was noticing stuff I didn't notice or appreciate before.

Never again.

It was as if I was entering a whole new world. Was this the end of the nightmare or simply the beginning of my new journey?

And then I saw them, my dream team: Mom, my sister and her husband and my ex-wife, Loreen. All standing there with tears running down their faces. I grabbed my mom and lifted her off the floor and held her so tight while she cried. I grabbed everyone else with my free arm and just hugged them as a free man.

I changed into the clothes they brought for me and then we left. As simple as that. I walked out and didn't look back.

I left sixteen years and eight months of my life behind me and walked toward the rest of my life in front of me.

No turning back, no turning back.

Release Day, November 24, 2009 with my mom and sister.

<u>Our Legal System</u>

There is a story to how I came to spend nearly seventeen years behind bars. It's not pretty either and telling it has a purpose. You see, I was wrongly accused and unjustly imprisoned for nearly half of my life. I was innocent and sent to prison for a crime I did not commit.

Our court system attacked me as completely as the woman I was accused of brutalizing. We both experienced consequences to our innocent behavior that changed our lives.

How could the best legal system in the world produce such a horrific experience for an innocent man? It may be the best but there are imperfections which produce a domino effect that can victimize victims and terrorize the innocent.

My desire is to bring light and focus to the forgotten victims of legal system errors in hopes of improving what we call the "greatest legal system in the world".

The Attacks

It was 1989 in Lake County, Indiana and there were a rash of attacks on who had to drive alone at night.

Between October and December, many women were being tricked into believing they had been in a car accident by someone who would intentionally bump the back of their car and pull over to assess the damages.

When the woman would get out of her vehicle, she would be attacked and robbed. If the woman stayed in her car and her doors were unlocked, she would be pulled out of her car and robbed.

These "bandits" were reported to be a group of five men. They attacked women of any race, as long as she was driving alone. Some reports said the men would go as far as having two get out of the car then one would check on the driver and one would pretend to check for car damages as well as check the passenger doors to see if they were locked. They used this as a way to get into the victim's car if necessary.

After about five robberies, the attacks intensified. The bandits began to beat some of the victims who wouldn't cooperate with their verbal demands. In some cases, the women were forced out of their own car and into another car with three of the bandits, while following the two who took the victim's car.

The woman would be reunited with her car after the bandits had taken everything they wanted from her vehicle.

Some women were lucky and smart. They were the ones who drove with all their doors locked and screamed as loud as they could. There were others who wouldn't stop until they got to a place of business or a lighted area with other people. These tactics would cause the bandits to speed off. The media began publishing this type of advice.

Gun shops reported an increase in gun sales as women began to buy firearms, take target practice and take self-defense classes in order to protect themselves.

However, this didn't stop these bandits. The attacks continued. Police departments in each city and town of Lake County, Indiana began to advise women to keep going if their car was bumped even though they didn't want to encourage leaving the scene of an accident as a general rule, but in light of the recent attacks police wanted to see that women were protected.

After this announcement at least seven to eight more attacks happened in the months of November and December that resulted in at least one woman going to the hospital with head injuries from being beaten and her purse taken. The attacks were getting increasingly violent as the month of December came in.

The bandits then became more vicious than "simple" abduction and robbery. The next victim was forced into their car, abducted and the group of men took turns raping her. The car used for this crime was later found and had been reported stolen.

These crimes had gone from purse snatching to robbery and abduction, beatings and now abduction, robbery and rape.

The police from several cities in Lake County,

Indiana issued another warning that the bandits were stalking women who drove alone. This warning came after two more women were reported to have been rammed from behind and robbed. But they were fortunate that the bandits were scared off because an on-coming car stopped at the scene before the bandits could finish.

All reports including these last two attacks described two of the men as black and in their early 20s. Most of the attacks happened between 11:30 p.m. and 2 a.m.

The next attack happened around 12:30 a.m. when a woman's car was bumped. As she got out of her car she thought it was very strange to see two men get out of the other car and moved toward her. She ran as fast as she could to the first house on the avenue and beat on the door to escape the bandits.

Another woman whose car was bumped the same night at 1:15 a.m. possibly avoided abduction and rape because she passed out while the men dragged her toward their car; she was treated at the hospital and released.

The last attack on December 6, 1989 was the most brutal of all. The woman was driving alone about 1:30 a.m. when her car was bumped from behind. When she got out to inspect the damages she was dragged into the bandit's car. The five men took her to a secluded area where she was repeatedly raped.

But this time the police believe their perfect crime spree was coming to an end because they left an "unusual garment" that would hopefully lead police to the attackers.

After the woman was attacked one of the men placed this garment over her head, then said, "Quick get her back into her own car." They took jewelry and a handgun that she had in her purse, shoved her into her car and they drove off. She took the garment off her head and drove home, called police and went to the hospital for treatment which included the completion of a rape kit.

The Arrest

On December 6, 1989, I was working the 3-11 pm shift at the steel mill. The day was memorable for me because of the complications that night after work that would haunt me for the rest of my life.

It started out as a good day. I mean, it was quitting time and payday and I was riding home with one of my co-workers. We met up with another co-worker and the three of us headed out to cash our checks before going home.

We were riding in a red 3-door 83 Ford Escort, as we left the plant. We decided that highway 80/94 would be faster. As we traveled on the highway, we began to have some car trouble. My co-worker had no idea what the problem was so we finally worked our way through traffic to an outside lane and got off the highway. The car finally died on the shoulder under the Georgia street overpass.

He got out and looked under the hood and shouted, "No oil". So we pushed the car about 10-20 yards from underneath the overpass further away from traffic.

It was a cold night, about 20' below with the wind chill and I thanked God I had dressed for the weather as we locked the car. We left two duffel bags and a brown grocery bag full of dirty work coveralls and took

9

off on foot to get someone to pick us up.

We began walking west on the highway toward the next exit. A State Trooper pulled up and asked if that was our abandoned car. We shouted yes and told him that we were going to call for some help. The trooper told us there was a phone on 25th and Broadway. As he drove off, we noted that he could have given us a ride. We continued to walk and talk quickly toward the Amoco Gas Station only to find that the door was locked. It was 11:30pm and that was too late for anyone to still come in. Now what?

Then we saw the phone that the Trooper said was on the corner but all we had was three un-cashed paychecks and not a coin between us. I searched and found an Indiana Bell credit card and called a friend hoping she was still up. I explained what happened and where I was so she could come pick us up. I hung up and told the guys our ride was on the way. We walked back to the gas station and waited, in the cold. Finally, we spotted her light blue and white vinyl top car making its way toward us.

I got in on the driver's side and asked what took her so long. As I drove off I told her that we'd take her home because of the cold weather and then I was going to come back and help get the car off the highway.

After dropping her off, we decided to go to a nearby liquor store where a lot of us went to cash our weekly paychecks so we'd have some cash to do what we needed to do. Sometimes we'd meet there and have a couple of beers after work but not tonight.

We made it to the store at about 12:25 am, just before closing time. The cashier even asked why we were so late because everyone else had been and left already. We informed her of our car troubles and she asked if we needed a ride because she was getting ready to leave work. We told her no but we did buy a 1/2 pint of Cognac and a couple of beers to knock the cold off.

We stopped on 21st Avenue and Grant Street which was a couple of buildings down the road and at about 12:45 am. I purchased $5.00 of unleaded gas and a quart of oil for the car we were in and a quart of oil for the broken down car. I put oil in the car while the gas pumped and we decided to take 21st Avenue to get back to the highway.

As I pulled up behind the stalled car, I told him to get into his car and I'd push him to Broadway and from there we'd try to get his car started. When he reached his car, I saw him motion something that I couldn't understand but he got into his car and waved his hand that he was ready. I eased into his bumper and began to push his car down the freeway to the Broadway exit.

He guided his car to the side of the road and I went down a little further and made a U-turn so that I would be facing his car.

As I got out of the car, he was yelling to tell us that, "Somebody broke out my damn window"! We went around to the passenger side of the car to see the broken window and noticed that all the bags were gone, 2 duffle bags and the paper grocery bag.

I said, "It's too cold to stand out here, so lets' try to get your car started and get it to your house".

We used my headlights to see to put the oil in his car then hooked up my jumper cables and waited about five minutes before the car started. He kept the car running while I unhooked the cables and closed both hoods.

I followed him to his house while he parked his car in the back. He told me he was going in for the night and would clean up the broken window glass and cover it with plastic in the morning.

"Let me know if you need a ride to work on Saturday, I should have the heat working by then", I said as I drove off. It was 1:10 am on Thursday morning and I still had to take my other co-worker home.

On our way we talked about how our green coveralls were in those bags and that we wouldn't be able to report them until Monday when the office opened. I dropped him off and headed to my apartment.

On my way home I saw a friend from out of town coming out of his mom's house and I stopped to talk. After a few minutes he hopped in the car and we went to an after-hours place for a drink. He went in to get some beer while I kept the car running. I told him about the night, the car that broke down, no checks cashed, the stuff that was stolen and no heat.

We drove to his sister's house and I finally relaxed, socialized and had a couple of beers. It was almost three in the morning when I left and went two blocks to my girlfriend's apartment. I told her about everything that happened as we settled in for the rest of the night.

When I woke up later that morning, the only thing on my mind was getting the heat fixed in her car. I dropped it off at the shop around noon and picked it up the next morning. I drove a heated car to work on Saturday morning. I used my spare coveralls for my weekend shifts.

The three of us went in early on Monday to see the manager and explain the lost coveralls. He said, "No problem, just sign this and I'll get you guys another spare". It was done and we didn't think about it again after that.

Christmas was a few weeks away and I was looking forward to a pay raise that would come in with the

New Year. Life was good.

I even remember helping to save a man's life on the job. His arm got caught in one of the conveyers and I was able to help pry him loose. I honestly didn't think twice about helping him because that was part of who I was. On Jan 2nd, the foreman came and told me there was going to be a safety meeting at the pump house office. At first I thought it was strange that the meeting was so late in the day, almost 7:30 pm but I wondered if management might recognize me for my quick thinking earlier in the day since we were big on safety.

When I got to the office I noticed that some of my co-workers were there. I listened while the plant manager talked about the safety hazards and attendance. Someone knocked at the door and the plant manager acted surprised when several men and a woman entered the room. I was beginning to think that they were company representatives coming to present me with a safety award.

The man, who began calling off names of people that I knew hadn't done anything out of the ordinary, finally said my name. I stood with a smile and walked over to introduce myself and was interrupted by him saying, "You're under arrest".

One of the other workers in the room was thrown to the floor and cuffed and two others were being cuffed, even as I was being hand-cuffed myself.

I was in total shock. I told them to quit playing games and that this wasn't funny. I thought the company was playing a joke until we go to the parking lot where several other men waited. I yelled, "What the hell are you doing to me"! But no one said anything.

I said, "The cuffs are cutting off my circulation"! Still, no one said anything. I kept asking and finally the driver said "Shut up boy, you'll find out soon enough. Just wait until we get your black ass to the police station, boy. "

I was thinking that maybe I'd better be quiet because the way this guy was talking wasn't too friendly at all.

Another man said, "You didn't think we would catch you, huh?"

"Catch me for what?" I said, wondering what was going on. "I haven't done anything, why are you arresting me, don't I at least have a right to know why you're arresting me?"

"You'll find out in a few minutes. We got you and you'll be put away for a very long time unless you cooperate with us." When we arrived at the police station I looked up and saw a man I'd seen before but couldn't place. They placed us in separate cells after the fingerprints and mug shots. We were shouting by then asking who knew what the hell was going on!

When the detectives came back I asked for my one phone call. I didn't know much about the law but I knew I was allowed to make a phone call. "Don't worry, you'll get your call but for now you just come with me", the detective said.

I followed him to a little room with no windows, a table and a tape recorder sitting in the middle. There were already two other men waiting to run some tests and ask a few questions.

"First, I need to know what I have supposedly done." I said.

The detective said, "Mr. Glenn, we already know that you were involved, we're just trying our best to help you out".

"Help me out with what?" I was baffled.

"We caught you red-handed and if you help us we

can make you a deal. We came to you first because you are the youngest and we know that you already tried to stop the other four men."

"Stop who? From doing what?" I asked. And then the light at the end of the tunnel suddenly and unexpectedly became a freight train.

"Come on, Mr. Glenn, you know you guys raped and robbed this helpless female on December 6, 1989 after you bumped her car. We also know that this wasn't your first victim, but this one we can prove and when we do, we'll prove that you guys are the bandits that have been terrorizing women in the area," the detective announced.

"You have got to be crazy if you think I had anything to do with those crimes and you're a damn fool if you believe I had anything to do with rape or robbery!" I shouted. "I've never taken anything in my life. I've worked for what I wanted since I was 8. So you've made a mistake and you have the wrong man. The last time I was in a car five deep with all men was probably in high school and that would have been me giving somebody a ride home since I was one of the few people with a car and a job. I haven't ever needed to take anything from anyone because I work for what I want. So you've wasted your time and the taxpayer's money".

"No, Mr. Glenn, we got the right person", as he looked straight at me.

Then he left and the other detective came in and we just had it out. He was screaming and pointing his finger in my face. When the other detective came in he had a pair of green coveralls in his hand. "Don't these look familiar to you, Mr. Glenn?" again looking straight at me. Aren't these your greens? Admit it, aren't they yours?"

I said, "I don't know if they're mine or not. Are these the same ones I had on when you took me from work tonight?"

"No, these are the greens you left behind at the scene of the crime." he said.

"I didn't leave any greens at the scene of any crime because I wasn't at the scene of a crime to leave them behind", I said. I was sure I was making headway with them. Surely they could see I was telling the truth.

"Well, we know that these are yours because you went to work and asked for another pair and this is your size."

It dawned on me that they could have been the greens that were stolen from the car the night we broke down on the expressway. I was sure that was the reason they were accusing me and as soon as I laid out all the details of that night, I'd be free to go.

"Mr. Glenn, where were you on the night of December 6th and who were you with?" I just figured since I had nothing to hide that I didn't have to remain silent. I told them, "I'll willingly tell you what I was doing and who I was with." So I began to explain what happened that night after work just to prove there was no way I could have possibly been at the scene of the crime.

The detective said "I'll check your story out but you and I both know you're lying. This is my last offer of help. If you refuse you're facing up to 120 years in prison. If I was you, I'd confess and work with us. Maybe you'll get a little jail time, maybe probation, but surely it'll be better than 120 years."

I told him "I'd given all the help I could possibly give by telling you the truth". "Look, I didn't commit this crime nor do I know who committed the crime."

The next thing he said just blew my mind. "We also have semen stains that belong to you Mr. Glenn."

"You couldn't have MY semen stains because I wasn't there to leave any!" This went on for hours before the detective said, "Get his black ass out of my face."

They took me to another room where I was given a DNA test which included head and pubic hairs being plucked and saliva. The nurse from the hospital assured me that if I didn't commit the crime, the DNA test would prove it so there was no need to worry about anything. After the testing, I was taken to a cell.

The sound of the iron bars being slammed shut and locked sent quivers through my heart. I called out to the other guys but no one answered. I started yelling, "When do I get my phone call?" Still no answer. I yelled again and finally heard the keys and a policeman telling me to come with him. Finally, maybe I was going to get my phone call or maybe they figured out it wasn't me but I was wrong. The police officer took me back to the interrogation room.

"Well, Mr. Glenn", the detective said, "We've got you."

We know that the five of you were in Mr. Daniel's green four door Pontiac.

"What? Who is Mr. Daniels? I don't even know who that is". I said.

The detective told me to stop playing stupid because the five of us bumped the back of the victim's car and attacked her when she got out to look and forced her in the back of the Pontiac. Three of us were in the car with her and two of us took off in her car and traveled to somewhere around the airport in Gary where we raped her. Someone was in the backseat all the time making sure her eyes were covered so she could not see the face of her rapist. He said I used the greens to cover her eyes at gunpoint before we argued who was going to rape her first. Then he told me that I raped her first and the other four followed and made her perform all types of sex acts even anal sex with her eyes covered the entire time and at gunpoint.

"Bullshit!" I yelled. "You got the wrong man!" This went on for hours until I was finally taken back to the cell to sit for what seemed like days until another officer came and opened the cell telling me to step out and cuff up.

That morning I was taken down a hallway where all five of us were reunited and shackled together as we walked out the hallway door to face the cameras with reporters asking if we were the bandits and why did we do it even as we were being shoved into the dark paddy wagon.

I started asking everyone what they knew but no one knew anything. When we came to a stop more people were shouting all kinds of names as we were lead out to the County Jail and locked in a holding cell.

It was at the holding cell that I saw the TV and learned that my face had been plastered all over TV as one of the bandits who had been terrorizing women on a three-month crime spree. I wanted to cry.

I was being portrayed as a monster without a conscience hurting innocent women. It was a lie and I knew it. I had already said it. But the lie was living a life of its own.

I shouted for my phone call again because I knew my mom and family would be nervous wrecks.
After 24 hours or more I finally made my first call to my sister who was in worse shape than I thought.

"What the hell is going on? You're all over the TV as this bandit, rapist". I told her I didn't do it and had no idea who did. It's been some kind of mistake. "You don't know anything about it?" she asked. Ok, I just needed to hear it from your mouth." And that was it. She believed me.

18

"You know there is no way in the world I could ever do anything like that. I was the one trying to get you and my girl to get some protection!"

Then I heard her and my mom on the phone asking if I was ok. Thankfully they knew I didn't have anything to do with these attacks. They knew me and they knew that I was working 16 hour shifts during some of the attacks.

They were already trying to get some money together for my bond which was $85,000 but I told them don't worry about the bond I'd be ok, just please get me a lawyer. I knew they would see me as soon as possible. My mom couldn't talk from crying continuously during the phone call.

County Jail

After the phone call, I was taken to section 3E with 47 other men. Everyone knew my face from TV and I thought I'd be fighting for my life but some of the guys knew people that I knew and had doubts about my guilt.

They just didn't think a guy working at the steel mill, making good money, would be out robbing people. And others just believed me when I said I didn't do it. But most of us felt that someone black was gonna pay for these crimes whether they did it or not. I just didn't think it would be me.

After a few weeks and some brutal fighting (none included me) the consensus was that I didn't fit the type that was being described by the police and media. But even so, I was still in jail.

My family was visiting me every week and the lawyer they retained for me was confident about the case except for the lab work that we were all waiting on that included hair and DNA analysis.

I had no criminal record, there were no eyewitnesses, and the green coveralls left with the victim had been reported stolen from the passenger window of my co-worker's car. Everything I told the police checked out.

But the crimes were continuing to be reported in the newspapers. "Copycats", the police said as we went into the 4th month of my incarceration.

One morning a guard awakened me for court. I was sure this was a mistake because my court date was a month away. But I got dressed and went to the court room where my family and attorney were waiting.

My lawyer asked me if I was ready to go home and I told him, yes.

I asked if they found the right guys and he said it wasn't your DNA at the crime scene or in the victim. The judge entered and said he would release me and only take a portion of the bond since I was indigent and a head hair found was consistent with me. He understood the possible transfer of the hair from coveralls but never the less with the DNA evidence I will release Glenn on a bond reduction.

The newspaper reported on April 26, 1990: *A judge released four men from jail Wednesday after the prosecution disclosed it has no genetic evidence linking them to a December car-bump and rape. The Superior Court Judge reduced the bond of two of the men from $85,000 to $25,000. He declared the other two to be indigent and released them without bond. Hammond police said the bandits rammed her car while she was driving near 165th Street and abducted her when she stopped to survey the damages. She was unable to identify her attackers because they pulled coveralls over her head. Prosecutors hoped to identify the attackers from genetic material found in body fluids left on pieces of evidence, but a forensic laboratory in Germantown, Maryland was unable to find genetic markers linking the defendants to the rape of the 28-year-old victim. Lacking a positive match to the defendants' genetic material, the prosecution dropped its opposition to bond release.* I wondered, even this early in the case, wouldn't someone in this group of men have left semen stains somewhere, if they participated in a rape?

There have been a series of similar car-bump, rapes since the defendants were jailed late last year. Defense attorneys said it proved the real criminals were still loose. Police have called them unrelated copycat crimes.

After those four months it felt strange going outside and home to a real meal. Getting back to work would be awkward after four months absent and a rape charge, but I had to put it behind me and move forward. My lawyer felt the case against us was given a blow by the DNA results and he believed that there might not be a trial at all.

The Nightmare

But there was a trial. Four months after my release after my life was pretty much back to normal, I got the call that the three of us would be taken to trial. I was stunned. I would be the last to be tried. The first trial was hung, the second was convicted and by then I was terrified.

I wanted to run but that's never been who I was. And besides why run if I didn't do anything. Even if the hair they found matched 26 characteristics of mine. And even if two jail inmates at the county jail said I confessed to being part of the crime. I knew I didn't rape anybody. I knew that the green coveralls were stolen. I had no choice but to fight because I had truth on my side.

The first trial in 1992 ended in a hung jury. It lasted about four weeks and at one point had my attorney serving as my witness. He testified that there was no way I could have allowed one of the jailhouse snitches to read my documents because he never gave me any documents.   His testimony placed doubt on my confession but then he could no longer represent me in the trial and since I could not afford a lawyer, one was appointed to represent me. The new lawyer fought hard and the jury could not decide. Again, I was told to go on with my life because there probably wouldn't be a re-trial.

But there was a re-trial. Three months later I got another call for another trial. My 2nd lawyer had resigned and was no longer available to represent me. I was devastated, furious and terrified at the same time. I had no idea who was going to represent me, who was going to fight for me, who was not going to allow me to be railroaded into prison. Who was going to believe in my innocence?

I was at a loss. I went from one attorney as my witness and liaison, another attorney as my mouth piece to nothing and no one.

I finally got a call from the lawyer who had been appointed to my case telling me to come to her office. We met and began making court appearances, requesting funds for more DNA and hair analysis experts as well as co-counsel because the case was so big in volume, evidence and in prosecutors - three to be exact with assistance from the lead detective.

But co-counsel help was denied and the trial was in 3 weeks.

My second trial was in 1993 and began the same as the first except this jury found me guilty of one of the three charges: guilty of Class A rape, not guilty of robbery, hung jury on deviated conduct.

The courtroom was in shock. The majority of attendees were family and supporters and all you could hear were screams and cries of No! This is wrong! He's no criminal! He didn't do it!

My lawyer even shouted out to the judge "No, your honor, this isn't right! It isn't consistent, there's no credible evidence!"

The only thing I really heard was the crying of my mother. Her screams seemed to be magnified. I looked around and saw people holding my mom and my sister trying to comfort them even as I stood dazed wanting to tell my mom it was going to be all right but just not sure at that moment what to think or do. Everything was foggy and blurry and seemed so unreal like a nightmare.

It had to be a nightmare because there was no way it could be real. Even as the judge told the bailiff to take me into custody, I was stunned.

I looked at my lawyer and said "You told me I wouldn't be convicted. Help me, please. I didn't rape anybody! I couldn't, I wouldn't rape or hurt anybody. Help me please."

She looked at me with sad eyes and said, "I will appeal. I'm not finished yet."

"I don't want an appeal", I said, "because I don't want to go to prison for a crime I didn't commit."

The bailiff was telling me to come on because I had to leave the courtroom. I did what I was told. The bailiff said he thought that most I would get is another hung jury.

He looked at me and said, "I'm sorry Mr. Glenn, a lot of us didn't see this coming at all." He had attended both trials and heard all the evidence.

Thirty days later I was in court for a sentencing hearing. My lawyer put up a tough argument for a lighter sentence than the 60 years that the prosecution was requesting. My lawyer said the evidence against me was fraudulent which gave me the opportunity to speak but even after that the judge said a jury of my peers had reached a verdict and he must pass a sentence. He would not give me the maximum but his sentence was 36 years because of the heinous crime that was committed.

I was ordered into the custody of the sheriff's

department to be transferred to the Department of Corrections to begin my prison sentence for a crime that I did not commit.

Reception Diagnostic Center

After two more weeks in county jail, I was transferred to RDC – Reception Diagnostic Center. It was almost like boot camp with everybody yelling orders with no questions asked. Everything was done in single file.

Single file going to chow, eating chow and leaving the chow hall. Two-man cells with no TV, radio, games, one toilet and one sink. We were allowed out of our 6x8 foot cells to watch TV for one hour every other day and to shower for 10 minutes at 4am every other day. We were being monitored and evaluated to decide what type of treatment we needed and the best prison environment we needed.

No phone calls or visits only written mail in and out. We wouldn't be in RDC for longer than 45 days. RDC felt like prison. Any foggy or blurry thoughts about it were turned into reality at RDC. It was the type of place that had you reaching down and pulling out any strength you had in you just to survive. It was a mental struggle just to stay in touch with reality.

As the counselors and psychologists began evaluating me, they weren't surprised to hear me maintaining my innocence because they heard it all the time. But they were surprised that at 31 years old, this was my first time in prison. They told me that in that case I would usually go to a low to medium security prison but because of the heinous crime committed they would have to send me to a maximum security prison. They chose Michigan City since it was closer to my home.

At RDC I initially did have one run-in with my Bunkie because he was an arsonist who burned things up when he got aggravated. I demanded he give up all his matches and lighters before bedtime and I refused to sleep in the room with him because he had just burned a building with innocent people in it and I didn't want to be next. I had to do things this way just to protect myself because I knew the guards wouldn't. Fortunately, things never got physical because he gave up his fire starting stuff and I searched him so I could sleep. I lit all his cigarettes and over the next 43 days we became sociable.

My name was called at about 3am on day 44 to pack up and head to prison. All kinds of chills went through my body and felt like I couldn't breathe. I was sure I was having a heart attack but it was just me feeling the pressure of prison.

Prison

About 30 of us were packed and loaded on a bus early in the morning. I was being driven away in a prison bus full of Indiana's most dangerous criminals to Indiana's most dangerous prison. Michigan City was the beginning of the most fear I had ever experienced in my life.

My life of following the rules and doing the right thing. My life of never committing a crime. My life. It was unreal that my life had somehow ended up here.

I wanted to die rather than face what was behind the walls of this prison. I looked up into the clouds knowing that only God could help me pull myself together. Only God could help me survive this kind of unfamiliar terror.

The first building reminded me of an old haunted house. We were escorted right through the center of the prison population in the midst of chow time as we entered. It was like a small city with all the sidewalks and roads filled with convicts yelling all kinds of things at what they called "fresh meat".

I started to shout back with words of my own when one of the guys with us said, "Shut up! Don't say anything.

He had been down this road twice before. He was pretty sure I didn't have anything to worry about as long as I didn't feed the fire, get in debt or act like I was better than everyone. "And don't mess with the boy IL NaNa",

29

he said. In prison when you use the word "boy" toward someone it stood for homosexual.

I started to meet people who had read about me in the newspaper. Normally rapists have it hard in prison, so I know God heard me because I also met guys who knew me as a kid who were important in the prison population. Others were gang members from different gangs and some who told me they were told to look out for me from family members on the street. Before I knew it a lot of guys surrounded me and couldn't believe I was convicted. Some knew me from school and knew it just wasn't in my character. They introduced me to a lot of people and wanted me to join one gang or another but I always answered "With all due respect, at my age and situation, I'll be joining God's Army." They accepted me and my reason not to join.

That's not to say that I didn't have a few run-ins and found myself carrying protection. I had seen some pretty brutal fights and stepped over bodies as well. I listened when I was told to keep my protection at all times in this environment.

During this time, Church was the most important thing to me.

Then one day while I'm sitting in my cell a guy yells my name and asks me if I know Anthony Glenn. "That's my little brother", I said. He slides the caddy down with a note that said Anthony Glenn was found dead, shot in the back of his head. I almost passed out. I didn't know how to respond. I felt like crying but didn't because I couldn't accept the words on the note. I shouted back that it must be somebody else, not my brother. He sent a second caddy with a note that said he was found by his mom on the stairs of their porch. She had been running hysterically down the street screaming when neighbors came out to help. The address was my mom's address. I shouted, "No, it's a mistake!" Just then my name was called on the PA system for a visit. It wasn't time for a visit so I just cringed and wondered who was coming to visit me and why. I prayed that it wasn't about my brother. But as the officer came to escort me, I could hear the sadness in his voice and I knew.

It was written all over my mom and sister's faces. "Is it true?" I asked. The answer unleashed the floodgates for all of us. Suddenly, I stopped and reminded us to lift our heads and keep moving forward and be strong for each other and for our children.

In that moment, I saw my mother's pain and realized she had experienced so much pain in the last few years. I just didn't want her to experience that anymore. I just wanted it to stop. I tried my best to show her that I would be all right. I wanted them to sense my strength over my pain.

I went back to my cell and asked God why this was happening to my family? Why us? Why me?

It was then that I decided that someone was going to pay. I decided that when that prison door opened, the first man to breath the wrong way toward me was gonna get it. I mean, if I had to be in prison, I might as well be in for a reason. Somebody was going to feel my pain. Well, that door didn't open. And I was still talking to God.

It seemed like another two weeks before that door would open. By that time I had a different attitude. God showed me that my anger and bitterness was destroying me and would only add to my mom's pain. I didn't want any parts of destroying my mom, my sister or any of my family. So when God got through showing me who I would be destroying the doors opened. I gave up the protection I'd been carrying and came out with a new attitude toward life and people. My language changed from what's up to hello. I didn't have any desire to use curse words of any kind or any kind of filthy communication. I was even walking around prison saying excuse me when someone else bumped into me.

Some wondered if I was all right but I was fine. I had a new way of thinking and living and it was effortless for me. When my family noticed the change, it meant the world to me.

This new spirit God put into me made my life easier on the inside of this prison system, but I never forgot that I was an innocent man in prison. Physically, no harm came to me and eventually I would be moving to a medium security prison.

This was more a mental battle and struggle for years and I'm still counting because mentally I don't know how badly I've been affected. Sometimes I think society will be the dictator of that because it is society who dictates what the norms are.

As an honest, hard-working, taxpaying citizen, I didn't deserve this treatment because our society is supposed to protect those who follow the rules, no matter the color or status in life. I pray that the day will come when our system will serve and protect all people and not be so concerned about notches in belts or playing games to see who can put on the best show for a jury regardless of the innocence of the accused.

Most people don't imagine that this could happen to their family, son, brother, husband, father, nephew, uncle, cousin, or friend. I was living a good clean life like most good people do, so if it could happen to me it could happen to anyone.

I knew this system in my county would need to be challenged by outside counsel not practicing in our area. While at Michigan City Prison I began to write letters to people all over this country, any type of law firm I read about that would help innocent people in prison. Sometimes I would see people on the news being freed from wrongful convictions and it gave me the hope that I would never let go of.

I told my sister to contact anybody she thought could help an innocent man in prison. I hadn't told her of all the things I was seeing and hearing all around me. My hope was to protect her and my family from any worry and concerns of my well-being. There were times when guys would tell me of the gruesome crimes they committed.

One of my "neighbors told me of how he ate human remains after killing and dismembering a family, another neighbor had committed multiple murders in a robbery. I was jailed with a man who used construction tools to beat someone's brain out of their head and another who used a microwave on the decapitated head of his victim. Then there were the two guys who heard voices telling them to open their victims head to eat the brain after killing them with gunshots.

And I really didn't want to tell my family about the guys I was around who continued to commit violent crimes while in prison. A part of me knew that my sister knew there were just things bothering me that I wouldn't talk about. We had a silent agreement. She knew, and I knew she knew, but I was committed to holding my head up and smiling every time I got a visit or talked on the phone especially with mom.

This was the struggle. To be in this environment that I did not choose or create with this violence, sickness and hatred and not become the environment. Sometimes it seemed like it would be easier just to let go and let the environment be my guide but I kept my faith in prayer and hope.

Michigan City Maximum Security Prison around 1995.

The Innocence PROJECT

Then one day I got some mail from an organization responding to one of my many letters. As I opened the letter I could feel my heart pounding in my chest. The letter said that my case sounded interesting but that they were unable to assist me at the time. However, they did refer me to an organization called the *Innocence Project.* They thought this group would be best fitted to look into my case because they deal with rape cases when DNA is involved.

A few weeks later I received a letter with *The Innocence Project* stamped on the envelope. Once again I was sure my heart was beating so fast that everyone around me could hear. This time they wanted the transcript to my trial and any other information I thought would be helpful in this case.

This was my sign that my prayers had been heard and I needed to never look back and doubt myself for choosing to live righteous in this environment. As soon as the cell doors opened, I ran to the phone to call my sister. She and her husband would have to be the ones to help with this task because to mail a copy of over 3,000 pages of transcript would take money that I simply did not have.

So arrangements were made for her to pick up the transcript from prison so that my sister could make copies and send them to *The Innocence Project.*

About six months later I received another letter from *The Innocent Project* informing me that one of the students that had been assigned to my case had ultimately decided that my case needed more attention than they could give at this time. They decided that because DNA testing had already been done and I was excluded, that more DNA testing would only exclude me again.

They noted that the serology test was allowed to include me even though the DNA excluded me and recommended that someone re-investigate this entire case from its beginning.

They also determined that the hair used against me at trial was allowed to include me because all 26 characteristics of the hair match 26 characteristics of my hair. It wouldn't be prudent to do a DNA test on the hair that my trial counsels thought may have been planted.

All of these areas needed to be investigated to its fullest. However, because they thought this was a wrongful conviction, they contacted a lawyer in Indiana who had reviewed the case and agreed to take the case pro bono on my behalf. They encouraged me not to give up on my fight for justice and to keep them posted on any new developments. They were confident that this attorney would do a great job!

But suddenly I had mixed emotions, not about my righteous living, but about whether anyone could help me. I rationalized that someone else believed a wrongful conviction took place and another lawyer took the case pro bono because they could see the injustice.

So now wasn't the time for mixed emotions, but a time to re-group and press forward with a positive attitude.

So I contacted my family and gave them the news with a joyful and confident attitude knowing they would feed off of my response.

Months went by and finally the lawyer in Indiana contacted me by mail. His letter confirmed his position with *The Innocence Project* and that he would be handling my case. It gave me a new hope.

It's been years and I'd been wondering when I could finally exhale. I just kept waiting and believing in my heart for the day when the sound of the CO's keys would mean freedom for me, that the mistake had finally been resolved and that I could resume my life. It was a fantasy but the lawyer's letter screamed "it could happen!"

For this lawyer to have taken my case pro bono must mean something. I thought He must have my best interest at heart but I began to question his motives and his dedication after several of my letters to him went unanswered.

When he finally answered, he said he was looking into some new case laws concerning the head hair and would get back to me after his research.

I had no choice but to wait patiently and stay positive even though this process seemed to be taking forever.

Prison ties your hands in so many ways. You are at the mercy of everything and have little influence over anything or anyone but yourself. It would be almost a year later when I heard back from him.

It was now 1996, three years after my conviction, and I was now in a medium security prison because of good behavior.

The lawyer contacted me because the detective on the case contacted my sister and she informed the attorney that the detective was willing to make a deal with me.

This letter was the lengthiest I've ever received from a lawyer. It was so gloomy my eyes filled with water before I was half way through the letter and it was the first time since my brother died that I felt tears sliding down hitting the letter as I continued to read.

This attorney was telling me my situation was hopeless and no relief would be possible for me. My best chance was to take the deal that was being offered by the detective.

This deal was for me to admit my guilt and flip on my co-defendant as well as another guy who was still on the street and working at the company who employed us. My sentence would be modified and I could possibly go home very soon.

I could not believe that was the offer! I rejected it immediately because I would not confess to a crime I didn't commit and I wouldn't lie on my co-defendant whom I knew also didn't commit this crime either.

My first letter was filled with all the anger and pain I felt inside me. I knew he had no idea what it was like to be unjustly accused and wrongfully imprisoned and encouraged to throw others under the same bus I'd been thrown under. I tossed the first letter and instead wrote to tell him that if he wasn't going to help prove my innocence then to let me be.

I figured that this lawyer had given up on the fight for justice because this was a real fight against a real enemy and was going to take real time, real effort, real money and because my county had threatened to use all of their resources to keep me in prison.

I felt like someone was squeezing the life out of me but I continued to pray faithfully to God. I just could not give up because I felt God had prepared me for whatever was coming my way. I would not give up; I could not give up. As my family continued to visit me I continued to show love, joy and peace in the midst of all I was going through.

My focus now was on the new location where I was being held hostage and the good treatment they give to those who follow the rules and guidelines. I became a well-liked convict at this camp. God was showing me favor for choosing to live and do right regardless of my circumstances.

My family was shocked at my desire and determination to live in love, joy, peace, and continuing strong in my faith. Another year had gone by and I was uprooted to another prison. I stayed there for four years.

I heard from the lawyer one time in that time but he wasn't my concern as in the past. It was as if my mind had thankfully gone to another place. I just didn't worry nearly as much as I use to. I was happier seeing that God was blessing my family; they had all become faithful members of their church.

God was also blessing me in that my ex-wife became the love of my life as though we had never been apart, and God had united us together through spirit and truth. Our hearts became one. She had been by my side since day one of my incarceration and God opened my eyes to see her in the spirit and in the natural as well. Through her I was being showed what love was and is and that it doesn't hurt, it doesn't fail, it's patient, it doesn't see fault, it only sees the good in all situations, even when things look their worst love still finds its best.

After the four years, I was sent back to the 2nd prison that God had shown me favor in. Although some of the staff members were gone by the time I returned, there were still many that I knew. I was given the same job as though I had never left. The staff wanted me in this high profile position because I respected everyone in the prison population and staff, without being a snitch.

I got respect and gave it to both sides. I was known as one of the guys not looking for any trouble, who loved to pray. And I did pray continually for everyone and for myself.

One Saturday morning my family visited as expected. But this time I could see pure joy on all their faces as I entered the visiting room. The smiles were glowing as they approached me waiting anxiously at our table. I hugged each one and wondered what was going on but no one said anything.

So, after we sat down, everyone looked at my sister including me. She could not stop smiling, and then she said "Ok, ok, I'm ready".

She said "I talked to a lawyer". I interrupted, "Yeah, how much they want and don't give them any money unless I say so after I have them checked out. You know the one guy is still my lawyer".

She said "Would you let me finish".   Ok.

She went on to say, "This lawyer told me to tell you she wants to come see you in person."

My eyes must have gotten big as half dollars. "Yes", she said, "she has paperwork for you to sign".

She went on to say that she wanted me to sign paperwork allowing her to represent me. I still wanted to know how much this was going to cost.

"Nothing. She is doing it for free. I didn't want to tell you about this until I knew it was going to happen. She is a law professor at IU Law School in Indianapolis, Indiana. She had been reading your transcript for two months and has decided that this case is a travesty of justice and she and her law partner agreed. Now she wants to make your case a school project for the wrongful conviction program here in Indiana".

My sister told me how she met the professor. After years of contacting members of the *Innocence Project* in New York a determination was made to refer her to a wrongful conviction program in Illinois. Six months later this program directed her to the wrongful conviction program in Indiana. After several phone calls were made to the Indiana branch concerning the referral she was then contacted by Professor Watson.

Professor Watson called my sister at work and although she was nervous she knew how important the call was for me. Her heart dropped as she listened to Professor Watson explain that she gets mail every day from people claiming their innocence. My sister had been down this road before believing that they would hear her today and forget about it the next time simply because she was my sister and she should think I'm innocent.

After an initial look at my paperwork, she and her students agreed my case was worth looking into further. My sister agreed to meet Professor Watson in a week in Michigan City to deliver the court transcript. At the meeting, Professor Watson was surprised at the sheer size of the delivery - 3500 pages of transcript - my life in 7 reams of paper - it took two men to transfer the transcript from the car to the van. The two women hugged and by this time my sister was in tears just sobbing, almost wailing in relief and in hope.

Professor Watson cautioned her not to get her hopes up too high. She reminded her that "I only said I would read them, I didn't say I would be able to get him out".

She knew it wasn't a done deal but suddenly realized that this was the first time she physically handed the transcripts to someone that she could touch. She apologized but she knew that I was suffering for nothing and before she knew it she had everybody crying.

She told Professor Watson, "I know my brother would have asked to be forgiven if he'd been part of this. But he has said from day one he didn't do it and he stands on that to this day 8 years later".

Professor Watson assured her that she would read them and let her know if there was anything she could do.

After two months, my sister got another phone call from Professor Watson while she was at work.

She apologized for taking so long but that it was a lot of reading. "Unbelievable", Professor Watson said. My sister asked, "Is that good or bad?"

Professor Watson's next words changed my life, "For

your brother it's good and bad because we don't believe he did it and it looks like there was just a bunch of bullshit done in this case. I couldn't believe some of the things I was reading so I had to get someone else's opinion as well and we both agreed this man is innocent. It was wrong that he was convicted of this crime and still sits in prison and apparently Lake County is not going to back down. So we will be climbing an uphill battle but we are going to fight for him".

She said, "Get in touch with him let him know were taking the case and that we need him to sign a contract. I'll be in touch with you later".

Thank you was all she could think or say. She and her secretary celebrated right there in the office. Soon she called her husband, my mom, my ex-wife and anyone else she could think of that wanted the best for me in this case.

My mom told her, "It was to her the best news she's had other than the birth of her grandchildren in 8 years of our suffering. This was a day she could celebrate and she did".

When she finally told me, I was speechless. This was the answer to my prayer. Someone outside of my family had heard me, they had listened to me and validated my experience. What a relief it was.

My sister had to remind me that I wasn't getting out next week, just getting a visit to sign the contract. "I know, I know, but do you know how it feels on the inside when a prayer has been answered in real time here and now. I've been praying for someone like this to help me prove my innocence every time I hear about it or see it on TV. And now it might be me."

<u>Leaving The Pain Behind</u>

Everyone at the table was teary-eyed and silent, cautiously joyful not knowing what the next moment would bring. Celebrating the occasion, enjoying the remainder of the visit that no one wanted to end. Just repeating hugs until finally the officers came over and said sorry Glenn, but it's time.

I gave my brother-in-law the most serious hug for all the love and support he had given me. My sister's husband was the only brother I had left and I vowed to never let him go.

Going back into the prison after visiting with my family reminded me just how lonely life really is without family and what they bring to this life that was forced upon me. The support of family was so important as I dealt with physical environments, lifestyles, circumstances and ways of thinking that were the complete opposite of normal for me.

Holding on to my family was one of the keys that helped me keep in touch with my core values. The values instilled in me as a child that grew with me through my youth and stayed with me even as an imprisoned adult. Their letters, visits and phone calls were food for my soul.

I will forever be indebted to my family for accepting the collect calls that devastated their phone bills. In my mind I was surrounding myself with positive influences, love, and common sense decisions and although my family may not have understood my need for them, they were one of the biggest factors in me becoming the man that I became.

Next to God, my family was the key to seeing me through these hardest, most unbelievable times of my life, and for that I must say thank you.

Within a week an officer came to my door and handed me a "call-out pass" for an attorney's visit. I was in shock even though I was expecting this day to come. The pass was for the next day at 10:00 a.m.

That night I tossed and turned all night and was up by at least 6:00 a.m. I had to shave and get myself together, because I was so nervous I could see myself physically shaking. I knew that this meeting would be one that could determine the next 10 years of my life. I didn't know what to expect from the professor and whoever was coming with her. The time had come for me to go, on my way the officers were wishing me good luck and told me to "just be Glenn" and this meeting would be all right. These were the officers I worked for and they could tell I was nervous.

While I was waiting several convicts passed by and asked why I was just sitting in the hallway. After telling them the situation they too gave me words of encouragement. Now, it was past the time of our meeting and I began to worry. I kept asking the officer on duty for the time. The officer told me they may have cancelled and she would call up front in ten minutes if they didn't show up by then. I said they'd be here only thirty-five minutes late.

Well, ten minutes went by and the officer called up front and found out there had been no cancellation.

Simultaneously another staff member from up front (officer dressed in street clothes, called my name.) I jumped up in excitement," Yes that's me".

She said, "You can come with me, your visitors are here".

I followed her to a secluded room and there were six people in there waiting for me. The staff member said we had complete privacy from this point on.

The professor stood and introduced herself as we shook hands then she introduced her five students and we each shook hands as well. As everyone was seated I remained standing and said "I'm Glenn, as you all know, and I want to thank each and every one of you for your time and this opportunity to talk to someone who believes in justice".

The professor began to speak with concern in her voice. That was so refreshing to hear from an attorney. "Mr. Glenn you don't have to convince me of your innocence, I wouldn't be here if I thought you were guilty of this crime".

I had to hold back the tears in front of these people, I had just met them, but, my God, she knew I didn't do it without even talking to me. Her confidence penetrated my heart so deep I wanted to just hug somebody. But I exhaled and said "Thank you. Hearing that means so much to me. It doesn't matter what happens from this point on. I'm just glad to know that someone can see for themselves that I'm not this person they have made me to be".

The Professor said, "Well Mr. Glenn I'm going to do my best to prove your innocence, but it won't be easy and I can't make you any promises other than I'll do my best. I've already talked to Lake County and they will not concede and plan to fight this case. They have to because someone will be in big trouble about this case should you prove your innocence in this late stage. But today we take it one step at a time and I have some papers for you to sign allowing me access and rights to any and all evidence, media, etc."

I signed the papers as soon as they were handed to me.

The Professor said, "I know you didn't read these contracts and for future reference don't sign anything else without reading it. I won't let that happen again".

I smiled, "It's just that I know you're heaven sent. This is my prayer unfolding before my very eyes. I prayed for years that someone, some university would come help me prove my innocence like I see happening for innocent men on TV and here you are".

"Well, Glenn my students will be using you as a school project and we will only work during school hours unless there's some type of development that needs my attention after hours".

She told me that the students had questions for me and that she would mediate and teach as they went along. This meeting lasted about three hours.

By the end, the students were surprised at my positive attitude and told me it was a pleasure meeting me and assured me that they would do their best on my behalf. When the session ended, I was real excited going back into the prison. It was great to know that I had competent help that had my best interest at heart rather than the state's interest, the court, the police, the victim or the community. She gave me the phone number at the university in case I needed to contact her. Once everyone found out that I had a team come to visit, questions began to come at me from all directions and mostly pulling for me. Man, was I excited.

A few weeks went by and I was ready to make my first ever attorney phone call. I told myself I would only let the phone ring a few times and hang up. The phone was answered immediately and my stomach began to make those nervous sounds and someone said, "Hello, Mr. Glenn how are you"? I was shocked. But I kept it together and responded as though I've been down this road before.

The voice on the other end continued, "This is Watson and we are working hard on your case. Your county is trying to be difficult as I expected. We are arguing over evidence which I know still exists, because my students have already been to Lake County's evidence vault and they have seen a list of all the evidence still available in your case. They went to your county as students doing research on old cases and how evidence is preserved. The evidence clerk was very professional and gave them everything we need on documented papers with signatures on them".

Professor Watson was having a conversation with me as though I was the one she had to report to. She made me feel important and encouraged at the same time. All I could say was thank you Ms. Watson. She began to explain how the prosecutors were going to make this a long drawn out battle over this evidence and that they were going to fight against every step she made. She also made sure to reiterate there were no guarantees. I told her that I understood and I applauded her for her efforts to prove my innocence regardless of any outcome. She told me as soon as she finished preparing for a prior trial and appeal that the necessary paper work for this case would be prepared and filed. All I could say was thanks for making me feel like I matter.

After this phone call, she told me to call once every other month to check in. There were times I would talk to some of the students about school, life, and how I managed on the inside. A rapport was developed between me, the students and legal administrators. These phone conversations carried on for about two years and by this time the actual case was filed in the court.

47

It was November 2003 (10 years after my conviction) and the petition filed alleged that there was false serology testimony including Glenn, when DNA excluded Glenn, ineffective on trial counsel, fundamental fairness. On March 11, 2004 the petition was amended and a hearing was set for October 14, 2005.

This hearing sparked a visit from the professor and the students. She came to discuss with me the importance of testing the pubic hair that had never been tested and to test the head hair that was said at trial to be a match to my head hair found on the victim's sweater. This head hair was believed to be significant in my conviction. DNA testing had never been administered to this head hair that was said to be a match to mine under microscopic analysis.

I immediately said to test it because I was sure of my innocence. I signed the necessary paper work and a staff member notarized it. Professor Watson reminded me that there was a possibility that the head hair could be mine if it was a transfer from the green coveralls that I had reported stolen or if it was true that this hair was planted by the detective as suggested by both trials counsels in both trials. But if DNA reveals that the hair used against you at trial is not yours as you believe then that would be strong and powerful evidence in your favor.

A few days later I received a transport order from the judge to go back to the county jail to attend an evidence hearing.

On October 14, 2005 this hearing became a fight because the state claimed that they could only find the pubic hair, which was not used against me at trial so it wouldn't matter about those results, and they didn't know where the head hair used against me was located.

Well, the professor produced the documents her students had received from the evidence clerk saying that this evidence did exist and the last known place of storage for this hair was in the prosecutors' personal evidence vault. The judge ordered that the pubic hair be tested and that the prosecutor produce this head hair for DNA testing.

The prosecutor claimed the professor was on a fishing trip. The professor says she loves fishing and she requested that the pubic hair be sent for testing today. The prosecutors objected saying this is not proper procedure, as they would need an expert to advise how this hair could be shipped in a professional manner. The professor says I have already investigated this matter and I have a scientific document from the science lab regarding their mailing procedure and protocol, and it states as follow: any evidence can be shipped to Cellmark Lab by a court in a secured sealed evidence container package and in a Fed-Ex sealed box. The professor then told one of her students to hand her the Fed-Ex box that was in her briefcase.

Once again the prosecutors objected saying this is good for theater, but not a court of law. The professor tells the judge that she also has the statue of law that states as long as the judge, prosecutor and defendant all sign off on the evidence that no chain of custody will be broken and the fact that this evidence has only been in the possession of the prosecutors and the court.

The defendant has no argument on signing off on this evidence. The judge ordered the evidence to be mailed by Fed-Ex and he would personally mail it himself. He ordered that we return on January 3, 2006 to conclude this evidentiary hearing and set date for a post-conviction hearing. It felt a lot like watching a tennis tournament with my past and my future as the ball.

Going back to the prison after sitting one week in the county jail was a blessing because doing time in the county is not on the top of the list of places to do time. Too many restrictions and no outside recreation.

Once I returned to the prison it seemed like January 3, 2006 came really fast. I was shackled once again and headed back to court. I didn't let the shackles affect me because it was part of the system and I understood it would take time to get me out of this system. Although it was humiliating as a human being, I knew that the people who had to do this to me were doing what they thought was right and it was their job. They had no idea that I was an innocent man. They didn't know I was just like them. That's why I strongly believed and tried to live Christ's words on the cross, "Forgive them for they know not what they do."

Getting back to the courtroom was a beautiful sight. Seeing my three children, mom, sister, and brother with a host of supporters filling the courtroom reminded me that there were many people who supported me and believed in my innocence. And I was really touched the moment I locked eyes with the love of my life who had been by my side since the day of my arrest. Even though she was happy to see me there was still sadness in her heart at my circumstances.

I smiled and embraced the students and the professor; we had all bonded like a big family. As court started I knew it wouldn't be long. The prosecutors produced everything left of the evidence including the one head hair.

We revealed in open court that DNA testing of the pubic hair excluded me. The judge recognized the exclusion as part of the record now and recognized all the evidence produced by the state was to be turned over to the university. The state noted that the head hair was too important to their case to allow it to be sent by Fed-Ex mail. They argued and it was determined that the evidence would be hand delivered by an expert of Indiana's laboratory who would also observe the handling and testing of the evidence. The Judge also ordered that the head hair be tested by McCrone and Cellmark Lab.

After two hours, the hearing was ending, another court date was set and I had to walk out of the courtroom watching the pain my family felt as they watched me shackled and hauled back to prison.

But this time we would be waiting on the most important evidence in my case. Every other DNA test had excluded me from the evidence presented in this case. The testing of this head hair was critical and this seemed like the longest wait of all.

By this time, I had been in prison for 13 years. The professor had requested two tests on the hair. One test would be another microscopic analysis to see if Indiana laboratory had it wrong. It was sent to the McCrone Lab in Illinois where one of the foremost experts in microscopic analysis reviewed the hair and determined that Indiana lab got it wrong in the first place. The hair was longer and thinner making any professional opinion to be at best inconclusive, but definitely not a match.

It was blatant to him as he viewed the hair under the microscope. He determined that the hair should not have been associated with me.

When the professor got this report she was a little excited because two characteristics were named that made it possible for the hair to belong to someone else. It was suggested that the only test available to get the most efficient result would be Mitochondria DNA testing. Professor Watson sent the results to the prosecutor and the court with a petition to move forward with DNA testing. This motion was also granted and the evidence was sent from Indiana Lab to Cellmark Lab. This total process took about a year.

Unpopular Move

While waiting, I also found out that all sex offenders would be sent to another institution for therapy classes. They began moving people to Miami Correctional Facility (MCF) quickly but as guys were being transferred many fights took place at MCF. The stories were being told that heads were being split open with weapons; eyes being blacken, jaws being broken. Although these stories were making a lot of people and families worried, I simply chose not to tell my family.

The stories made me nervous but I wasn't afraid. I was just hoping I didn't get put with someone who would be attacked because I might have to help that person and that was my biggest fear.

It was my turn to move in August 2006 and I still had no word on the DNA results of the head hair. As I packed, I couldn't help but think that I was tired of moving from joint to joint. This would be my 4th prison and 5th move in 13 years.

Arriving at MCF was exactly what I thought it would be. Officers mad at you because they've been told and believed everybody was a child molester. Child molesters have always been subjected to the worst treatment prison had to offer. Even though this was how I was perceived, I continued to be peaceful, joyful, and respectful. Always praying that God would see me through and show me favor. I saw guys I'd known since my first day in prison 13 years ago. Some even remembered my name.

I went to what's call P. House it was supposed to be the worst. The place where most guys were being robbed and beaten. I took a deep breath as I entered the building and went to my new two-man cell.

My Bunk-mate was a gang member from my hometown in Gary. He was young and trying to get out of the gang. He began to tell me about the different guys who were being jumped when the doors open for chow. Before I knew it, I began to talk in an attack mode but then this youngster stopped me and said I don't want to fight you. He said I don't think like them guys. I want to change my direction because I don't want to come back to prison. I had to come to myself and apologize. I explained that I had my guard up in here because of all the stories about how you non-sex offenders are pounding on sex offenders. The sad news here is I'm not even a sex offender or any offender. I've been fighting a wrongful conviction since I've been here.

Then the doors opened for chow and I stepped out not knowing what to expect. But glory to God I knew faces in this building and they knew me. Again the handshakes, the conversations, and one guy even asked are you still in prison from that same case. I said yes and he said "Man that's BS but it looks like you held up well".

He told me, "I know you heard about all the stuff going down but you don't have to worry about that because when you see the guys doing that mess you already know them and the Aryan's can't touch you. I told him that I wasn't worried much about me but I was concerned about some of these guys I know getting beat up. This needs to stop. He told me that the only thing I needed to worry about was myself because I knew how it went in prison by now.

I just began to pray for everyone who was labeled a sex offender. In prison sex offenders were literally labeled on their forehead by D.O.C.

My first line of business was to give college a shot. I wanted to go but even the word "college" just seemed intimidating since I hadn't been in school over 15 years. I dove in and began to see that at 44 years old I could do this if I applied myself.

Months later some of the law students visited me. I always appreciate their encouragement. My first semester was going well and the students were happy to see I was still going strong.

They were ready to attack the court as soon as the results were returned from the testing of the hair. Since I was so hopeful of my upcoming court date, I withdrew from college. I couldn't keep my grant if I missed days and court would mean missed days. I wanted to be prepared but in the end it was a mistake because the court date didn't come. Even though I jumped the gun, I was able to re-enter for the Jan 2007 semester.

Excluded

It was another new year. I'm always thankful for the New Year because it's one year closer to my out date. I re-enrolled in college and school was going great. By April 30, 2007 the head hair results were in and it was an exclusion.

The hair they said was a match to my hair wasn't mine at all. It didn't even belong to anyone related to me. We were all excited! The professor and students celebrated and my family cried and celebrated. I shouted while I was in the cell by myself. This was a great day but I knew it wasn't over.

The prosecutors would not just lay down and roll over because it would make them look unethical and incompetent if I won this case. On November 19th, my attorney filed the paperwork requesting a new trial. She amended the petition for post-conviction relief with the head hair result attached.

On Feb 11, 2008 the hearing was set for March 17-18, 2008. This was the moment I'd been waiting for. My chance in court to prove my innocence ... 15 years after the fact.

This time I didn't withdraw from school because the court dates fell during spring break.

Post-Conviction Relief

The fact that the head hair used to convict me wasn't mine at all would be the highlight of the upcoming hearing. But I knew the professor was right when she told me there were no guarantees. Even with the new evidence things might not change.

I wanted to believe that there was no way our government or the courts would allow false and incorrect evidence to keep me convicted. So once again I trusted "the system" to do the right thing, to do the thing it was designed to do. This was my hope, the hope of my team, my family and my supporters.

Five days before the hearings were to begin, I was transferred back to Lake County. Once again I went through the process of booking at the county, a new photo, finger printing, paperwork, being stripped naked and searched, showering and being issued a new set of clothing and all this after sitting in a holding tank with 20 to 30 other men for four of the five days.

Some men remembered seeing me before in the County, some heard about me from family members, and some read about the case in the newspaper. Some of the guys believed in my innocence while others questioned my innocence.

But one thing everybody could agree on was that 15 years straight in prison on a questionable conviction deserved to be released with this new evidence.

I really was shocked at the attention that my case was receiving. I knew an article had been written by my family and attorney but I just didn't give it that much thought. However, I got the full effect when the officer escorting me to the courtroom began telling me about the number of supporters and even media waiting in the courtroom. He wished me the best and wondered how I made it through 15 years without cracking up or falling apart.

"Honestly", I told him, "Prayer, hope and the belief that God would see me through. And I'll continue to make it through regardless of what happens in this courtroom."

By the time we reached the courtroom the officer decided he would take the cuffs off before I entered rather than leaving them on me as I entered. That one act meant a lot to me and I thanked him for his consideration.

The courtroom was an amazing sight. The law students who were seated in the jury box stood to shake my hand. Professor Watson met me in the center of the court and the rest of the courtroom was ridiculously packed with family in the front, reporters close by and supporters filling the room to standing room only. The professor introduced me to the reporters as I sat down.

This encouraged me a great deal, this new evidence must have a lot of people believing in me and hoping for my release. The professor was shocked at the support too. There were people in the hallway who were here to support me as well. All I could say was "My God" as I waved and acknowledged the people including some of my friends from childhood. I couldn't believe how many people were there. My family gave me a thumbs up and I was in overload.

The judge entered and the formalities began. Our first witness would be a scientist, a doctor with a specialty in forensic biology, genetics, and human DNA. His testimony was the most favorable information that I have heard in this case and in my mind it set the stage for my release.

Finally, this would be the time of my vindication and freedom. This time everyone would know that I didn't rape anyone. I sat next to my attorney with nothing but confidence.

I knew what evidence was against me: a pair of coveralls that I reported stolen to the company I worked for after a co-worker's car was vandalized while stranded on the highway. Then a state trooper testified about talking to the three of us as we walked away from the stranded vehicle and when the co-worker's car was confiscated by police the window was broken out just like I reported to detectives.

Then there were these jailhouse snitches whose testimony shouldn't have been credible because the professor revealed their testimonies contradicted each other. They gave two different accounts of what happened to the victim even after I had denied ever telling anyone that I was involved in the crime. It was also shown that their testimony even contradicted the victim's testimony. If you believed either of them, then the victim's testimony could not be believed.

And finally the victim stating that, even in the beginning, she couldn't identify anyone involved and that no one was ever picked out of a line up or photo array and that she never identified me.

The professor argued that all of this evidence that had been previously presented should be viewed as argumentative disputing points of fact. At best, very weak circumstantial evidence, which could be used legally to convict, but that was not as powerful as factual evidence, which we were about to present.

I was sure that the circumstantial case against me had been shattered, because the strongest piece of evidence was the head hair used against me and that was proven not to have come from me.

All this information was running through my head as the first witness was called. I was hoping no one would notice me having an anxiety attach right there in my seat. I had to calm down and breathe.

The doctor's credentials were not disputed by the state. The professor then asked about his opinion of the validity of exhibit 56 (which is a wall size chart purported to be a genetic marker chart and contained serology results).

This chart was used as an aid to presentation. (Serology is a science of blood. This technique was used before DNA testing was developed, it gives you statistic like: 1 in 1000 or 2 in 1000 etc.)

He confirmed that on this chart Glenn was included in a stain left at the crime scene and the serologist also testified that she could not exclude any of the three men with her blood testing from several stains even though DNA excluded them. He confirmed that the serologist also testified that she had some training in DNA testing as well and that serology is more sensitive then DNA.

So now, 15 years later, I would get to hear what a scientist had to say about the testimony given by the state laboratory when I was convicted in 1993.

The professor asked if he could dissect Exhibit 56 line-by-line in terms of interpretation and presentation.

He starts by saying: "*It appears the science was done well in this case in terms of the laboratory. He goes on to say that he has a big problem with, the interpretation of the results and the presentation of those results and those leads to problems that you can decide. Let's go to the first piece of evidence the vaginal/cervical swab. As I understand in this case, the victim was inseminated by a number of men, according to her testimony. The swab, K.E. testifies has material positive for semen. So, they recover semen from a victim of a multiple rape. And it's a very important piece of evidence. It's processed as best I can tell, very, very, well, and so I agree with all of the findings until we get to the statistics. I don't know who put those on there (the chart) and I don't know what they were trying to show, but it is extremely misleading.*

See the *Serology Genetic Marker Summary Chart* used in the 1993 trial that resulted in conviction. State's Exhibit no. 56, consisting of a serology chart that is being held in the custody of the Superior Court of Lake County, Criminal division, until the termination of the appeal in this cause.

Figure #1 gives you each person's blood type and frequency found in groups of people. Glenn is shown as having type O, with the markers 2 –1, 2+ 1+, 1. This chart puts Glenn in a blood group.

Figure #2 shows semen stains found on items of evidence. KE told the jury in 1993 that Glenn was included in stain 3 1 and could not be excluded from any of the stains because of his markers found in the stains with no objection from his attorney. Today, we know that these markers identify groups of people not individuals. DNA testing has now revealed that Glenn has been excluded from all these stains, something a jury should now know.

The professor says, "Why? Tell the judge why."

The doctor continued, "*Because in a piece of evidence, what I want to know is if I took the phone book of the town that this happened in, how many pages do I get to eliminate by that piece of evidence? If everybody's included, it's an inconclusive piece of evidence. Doesn't tell me anything. So what I want to know is what fraction of the population is still included as a possible contributor to this stain.*

"We already know it contains semen. Women do not produce semen. It's a mixture. By definition, it's a mixture. There are two ways to approach this both of which I think would be fine. One of them is to say "Gosh, look at this. It's exactly like who?" The victim. Standard forensic practice would be to say that's inconclusive. When you take an intimate sample from the body cavity of a victim of a crime and all you get is the victim, it doesn't tell you anything. Non-informational. Now what the examiner does in her report is absolutely amazing to me in that she says the seminal stain on the vaginal cervical swab for item two, demonstrates the presence of B and A, blood groups, that's true; PGM type two one, true; PGM sub type two minus, one plus; Pep-A type one. She calls it correctly, and then she interprets it. And she says, "This is consistent with a mixture of body fluids from MW and BJ". This report was turned by someone into this chart. Now, what we could do is say, "Well, you know what all that we found was the victim, and so it's inconclusive. But you can't have it both ways. In the report that's what they do and it's mirrored on the chart. In fact, whoever prepared this chart goes further by preparing an inclusion when this should have been exclusion. This man is excluded from this sample. This statistic of the victim on this line has nothing to do with an evidentiary analysis. So, there's nothing about this chart that is right, and it's horribly misleading. This is the most important piece of evidence. It's a semen stain inside the vagina of a victim who's just been raped."

So, what do we have in item three-one? What we want to know again is specifically what is left off this chart. Why did they not calculate the most probative statistic? There are meaningless statistics. I don't care how rare your profile is, I care how informational is this stain. Who's included in this? Well, who's included in this, Your Honor? I assume you are. This is the stain the chart told the jury Glenn was an inclusion and couldn't be excluded by serology testing.

The problem is that any expert at the time of this conviction in 93 and she had some training in DNA, but in any case, any scientist at the time who worked in the lab, especially a lab who just sent a sample off to Cell mark would know that the expense and difficulty of preparing and sending a sample to Cell mark, was more than paid for by the specificity of the test and the question about sensitivity becomes moot once there is sufficient material to be tested. It's like an eye chart you know if you see it you don't need a telescope. If you can see it with glasses that's good enough. Don't buy a telescope, wear your glasses. So if there's enough DNA, enough material to get enough DNA to get a test, DNA is by far a better test.

You're not going to get these every-white-person-in-the-world-included type results if you use the DNA test. And I think that point is obfuscated by the repetition of this statement, and it's several times brought up and in closing that serology is more sensitive. As if sensitivity has a value, once you have enough material, and actually it has no value. Once you have enough material to test, then you should always go for the more specific test. But her testimony was that Glenn could not be eliminated from any of these stains: Items # 3.1,3.2,3.3,3.4 by her serology testing."

Professor Watson says, "Now Doctor, what's the relevancy of a serology inclusion when DNA RFLP testing excluded? To present this serology as inclusion, in light of that DNA evidence, is disingenuous, at best. An expert of the day would know that the reason they sent it off for DNA analysis was because this serology is a very weak tool in these mixtures, and particularly in the mixtures in this case, whereas, the DNA would be a very discriminating test. I just went to a class on mixtures on DNA run by the American Academy of Forensic Scientists a few weeks ago. Even with DNA, which gives you all these great statistics in fact, in a majority of cases, as I recall the study, if you have four people it will reveal no more than three in most cases, even with DNA, because there's' so much overlap. All that demonstrates that when you have a mixture, picking our individual is going to be a very dicey business, and the best you can hope for is to eliminate people who are not there, but in terms of saying that someone is definitely there because their markers are there it gets dicey. Fortunately, in this case there's a clear exclusion. I mean that's highly unlikely in a group of where there's five contributors, plus victim, to exclude somebody, that's very important. That's a very significant piece of evidence.

So if an expert receives DNA exclusion as to item of evidence 3.1, can you explain their relevancy of a serology inclusion? "

The doctor responded, "*No, that's like saying the blurry, fuzzy picture of the moon, versus landing on the moon and getting it in high detail. You should trust the more discriminating scientific results. That's why you pay for the more discriminating scientific result. In fact, this is very clear in that there are no bands, as referred to, I think, in closing arguments that don't include the suspects.*"

There are two patterns: Two actual DNA banding profiles of RFLP that still doesn't include either of the suspects. And on two separate pieces of evidence they find the same patterns. So here we have a really great piece of evidence for the day. You have this jacket with semen smeared on it in several places. You actually get DNA extracted in the early 1990's. You have enough to do RFLP, which is still very robust statistically. Just as strong as any strong DNA result. And they get banding patterns that aren't the victims from semen stains that are very specific, and they exclude. And those exclusions are absolute. With DNA the exclusions are absolute. It's not a question of 90% of the population, etc. They are not there 100%.

Professor Watson then asks the doctor what is his

opinion about the previous testimony when she was under oath made statements about inclusion by serology when DNA had excluded as to the same stain?

"You know I'm baffled. I don't know. I wish I had an easy answer as to why. The only two obvious choices I have are absolute incompetence and the other indicates malfeasance. I don't know what else to say. It's clear that the data is good. She has the reports from the best people in the country. Her (K.E.) own data excludes him weakly. At best serology should be inconclusive. It isn't exclusion and it is certainly not by any stretch of the imagination, an inclusion though. Then you have this beautiful DNA that she requested they send her the results and they are 100%. I mean every one of them 100% excluded. I don't know. I don't know what to say. I don't get it."

"Does anybody use a serology test following a DNA exclusion for any value in terms of identity?" Professor Watson asked.

"I can't think of a case, either in my practice or historically in the literature where that would be probative, no.", as Professor Watson finished with the witness.

As the scientist left the courtroom I was shocked at what I thought was a powerful testimony on my behalf and as I looked around the courtroom I got the impression all my supporters felt the same way.

My attorney looked confident, but she reminded me as we made eye contact that there are no guarantees. I still believed that the science just revealed an injustice and definitely unfairness.

Now before moving onto the next expert witness, let me try to put some things in their proper perspective. My jury consisted of no experts in science or serology or DNA, but a jury of my peers. So, I was sure that after hearing the initial testimony they either thought I was a contributor to these semen stains or they were confused with the DNA versus serology as it was explained because I know I was confused.

Now, at my original trial normal people like you and me were left to decide on the testimony and being that normal people sitting on a jury could only use what God blessed them with, which is their common sense and gut reactions they chose to believe that I must have been a contributor to the semen stains according to the guilty verdict they reached.

I'm not mad at them because they had to make a decision based on the evidence presented at the trial but now after hearing the testimony of a scientist using today's technology the question was would I be given a new trial?

As I sat there listening to the conclusions and wondering what the jurors who convicted me would say. Would they have found me and my co-defendants guilty or innocent if they had truly understood the report and what it really meant?

I did not have long to ponder that before the next witness was called. She was a co-worker of the examiner prior to her death. I did not know what to make of why Professor Watson subpoenaed a staff member who worked at the state lab with the very scientist that testified against me.

I never questioned Professor Watson because I knew she was heaven sent and had my best interest at heart. But I did wonder at this one. So, I just began to doodle on a piece of paper to settle my nerves as the witness took the stand. She was in the courtroom for the previous testimony. Professor Watson verified that she heard the testimony and if she agreed with it. She said she agreed in relevant matters.

Professor Watson began a series of questions:

Q. Were the serology results misleading in the face of that DNA results?

A. If you didn't know the DNA results, yes it would be.

Q. Suppose you didn't understand the DNA results?

A. Well, then it's up to somebody to explain it, I guess.

Q. She testified to inclusions by serology in the face of DNA exclusion. Do you agree with that?

A. She was testifying to her results. She was not qualified to testify to the DNA results, and so all she was able to do was testify to the results she obtained herself.

As I listened I realized she was a hostile witness looking to undermine my attorney, but I wasn't giving up yet. My attorney wasn't finished either because there had to be more information this witness could provide. So as I began to squeeze my ink pen anxiously waiting for the next question.

Q. I am asking you would she have known in your opinion, that her serology results were inconsistent with the DNA results.

A. If she would have known the DNA results, yes.

Q. She would have known that the DNA results excluded Glenn?

A. Yes.

Q. And so she would have known when she said to the jury under oath, when she said "serology puts him in that stain," she would have known DNA took him out of that stain?

A. She would have known that, yes.

Q. If you have a DNA exclusion today, would you ever do a serology test on that same stain?

A. I don't know of any forensic lab that does serology testing anymore.

Q. She testified in 1993?

A. Yes.

Q. And the crime happened in 89?

A. Yes.

Q. And a lot changed in DNA in that period, right?

A. Yes.

Q. And so when she comes to testify in 93, that's years after her result.

A. Yes.

Q. And so she did her serology test before the DNA test?

A. Correct.

Professor Watson states, "The witness has affirmed what Glenn has claimed all along, that the initial testimony that stated Glenn could have been a contributor to item 3.1 and that she could not exclude him from other stains, was a lie."

I was stunned and thought to myself, Man, is this real? I mean this lady knew I was excluded all the time, while she testified to a jury that I couldn't be excluded?"

It hurts. To know for a fact that this lab cheated me, and this testimony was coming from one of their own. I'm glad she told the truth in the end, although reluctantly.

There would be one more witness for the day (the 17th) and we would conclude the hearing the next day (the 18th). The next witness would be the trial attorney who represented me at my 2nd trial, which lead to my conviction.

As the attorney took the stand, we both gave a friendly look and nod to say hello without speaking. Professor Watson always believed that she didn't have enough help to defend me and didn't' investigate the prosecutors evidence in order to make reasonable decisions which prejudiced me.

The professor began by stating:

Q. Drawing your attention particularly to the serology testimony if you will, if you'll remember back to this trial.

A. Yes.

Q. And you remember the DNA results, which you admitted into evidence?

A. Yes.

Q. And there was also serology testimony at the time if you know, why did you not object to the serology testing?
A. Well to be honest, I trusted the results that were provided by the state as the state evidence. I believed it came from the state lab, and I believed it to be trustworthy. I believe it to this day. I did not trust the detective involved in this case. But in terms of the state lab, I just didn't' think it went that far.

Right now I'm sitting in court thinking that my attorney trusted the very people who were against me, and even though my life was on the line (at the time I faced 120 years if convicted) she chose not to further investigate into the prosecutor's serology and microscopic hair analysis evidence which would have allowed her the opportunity to properly cross-examine about the supposed 26 characteristics that matched my hair and the serology testing.

I sat there thinking to myself, "You didn't object because you trusted the prosecutor's evidence". I am hoping she can read my eyes because they're talking to her. She could have objected to the prosecutors' reliance on serology and clarified for the jury the significance of DNA exclusions.

She said that she didn't understand that the previous testimony was irrelevant in the face of DNA testing which excluded me from being a contributor to the semen stains found on the victim's jacket and sweater.

She made a big mistake in not objecting to the evidence, a mistake that cost me my freedom. She trusted the evidence of the prosecutor and I trusted the state to do the right thing as well. Should the court continue to hold me responsible for her mistake? If so, the court has lost sight of the intent of our forefathers whose goals were to impose justice with fairness.

After she stepped down from the stand the judge confirmed that we had no more witnesses and recessed until the next morning.

I went back to my section confident that this was a very good day for my defense team. They all seemed to be very happy about today's events, the students were all smiles and my family looked like a lot of pressure had been released.

The biggest surprise before leaving the courtroom was the concern shown by my previous attorney who had stayed in the court after her testimony and gave my family hugs and support. She called my name as I was headed out of the court, caught up with me and gave me a hug as well and we exchanged friendly comments. We both smiled and walked away.

I'm not allowed to touch my family during these hearings but lawyers are ok if they so choose.

As I lay on my bunk guys would walk by with encouraging comments. All I could think about was tomorrow and what might be or might not be. I tossed and turned all night long, it seemed as though this was the longest night I'd experienced in my life. But finally it was morning. I ate breakfast, shaved, showered, and got prepared for my name to be called.

Finally, it was time, the officer called me cuffed me and escorted me to the holding cell down the hall from the courtroom. I was put in a cell by myself, across the hall was another cell with about 10 people waiting for normal morning court call. I had to wait for everyone to finish, then my hearing would take place. These cells were dark and smelled like raw sewage and the toilet and sink looked like raw sewage.

After about two hours, it was time for my final hearing day to show why I deserved at the least a new trial. Entering the courtroom, I noticed all the same faces as though no one had gone home but with one difference. My attorney's facial expression wasn't the same as yesterday and that instantly concerned me.

As I was being un-cuffed, I asked if everything was okay. She said yes, but one of our experts couldn't make it due to illness. He was supposed to fly in from Texas. His laboratory, Cellmark Diagnostic Center was the best in the country and did all the DNA testing. All I could say was you got to be kidding me. She told me not to worry we will get him here one-way or another.

We had our hair expert in the courtroom and he would be our next witness. This doctor's testimony was very important because of prosecutor's expert who was qualified as an expert witness in the field of hair comparisons and analysis at my trial. She testified that she found several brown hairs that matched the victim's hair. She testified that she found one dark hair, which obviously did not come from the victim.

She stated that the one dark hair matched the hair of Glenn. She stated that Glenn's hair sample matched 26 characteristics of the hair found on the sweater. She stated that Glenn's hair had unique characteristics that she believed to be significant in her conclusion that the two hairs matched. She found that because of the unique characteristics that she found in this hair that it would be very unlikely that the hair could come from someone else.

The judge asked for our next witness who, was identified as one of the foremost authorities in the field of microscopic hair analysis, his credentials were not disputed by the state.

Q. Did you have a chance to review the hair evidence in this case?

A. Yes.

Q. And did you also review the testimony.

A. Yes, I did.

Q. What is your overall opinion about what you reviewed?

A. First, let me say hair analysis techniques have not changed since the time of the initial work. Clearly, the hair taken from the victim's sweater should never have been called of common origin with Glenn. It was, in fact much longer and finer than Glenn's. The scientific consensus is that, in order to conclude that two hair samples could have a common origin, it must be determined that there are no significant macroscopic or microscopic differences. A single significant difference between the two is a strong indication of two sources given the fact that the head hair was dissimilar to the known sample from Glenn. I tried to suggest that there's really no value in the hair association that was testified about in court and that the likelihood it could have come from somebody else.

Q. Why did she get it wrong, in your opinion?

A. Well, I suppose there are three or four possible reasons. One is that she just was not visually literate, didn't have the acumen to see features. It's also possible she made the whole thing up. And it's possible she simply misused the language, misunderstood the language or the concepts and language that's appropriate in doing this work and testifying about it. It is my recommendation that this hair be analyzed for mitochondria DNA. Without DNA analysis there is no way to know from whom the hair originated from.

I sat there in total shock. I looked at the judge half expecting him to say, Okay. I've heard enough and it's time to let this man go home after hearing these scientist's reports and opinions.

After he stepped off the witness stand the professor says, "For the record both parties have signed off and stipulated to the MT-DNA testing that was done by Cell mark lab. This type of testing became available in the late 90's. Mitochondria DNA testing of the lone head hair off the victim's sweater has established that it was not from the head of Glenn, which supports the doctor's testimony."

She continued, "At this time your honor, my other witness could not make it today do to an illness. Can we now reschedule this witness because his testimony is important to this case?"

After a few minutes of arguments as to the importance of this testimony which the court and the prosecutors thought was not necessary, enough DNA testimony had been put on however, a new date was set after the scientist was contacted by cell phone in open court. The new date was set for June 24, 2008.

At this date the judge ordered all evidence be final and closing arguments be prepared because he believed he would make his decision on that date. Professor Watson also informed the court that she would be sending out subpoenas for the prosecutors who prosecuted this trial to find out who made the chart used in the courtroom and did they know this serology testimony was false inclusions in the face of DNA exclusion or the fact that they should have known.

You could hear some disappointment in the audience for the length of time between court dates. I wasn't too happy about it either. I had no time to talk to anyone other than to say see you later. I couldn't talk to my attorney either. So for me it was back to my section for a few days and back to the prison.

On my way back to prison I thought about college to get my mind off the case, and how it was spring break and I would be back in time to complete my 3rd semester. I was blessed to get back in time for school and I even got back in the same building that rarely happens. I had five classes and really had to focus during this third semester. I ended the semester with a 3.2 GPA. I had hoped to do better but under these circumstances I accepted it with hopes of doing better during my final semester of earning my Associates Degree in general studies.

Time was moving fast, school was out and I kept busy in the weight room. Early morning, around 1:00 a.m. I was told to pack for court a week ahead of time. I laid awake all morning going over everything I could think of to convey my innocence. I was carrying on as though I was the attorney and the professor was my assistant. My brain was running at a speed high above the norm. It was moving so fast my thinking was getting cloudy because there was no way I could do what I watched the professor do. Before I knew it my door slid open, it was about 7:45 a.m. and time to go.

The Decision

It was actually inspirational going back to the county jail this time because I heard much positive evidence and I knew this would be my time to finally get the shackles off once and for all.

In spite of the harassment of the county's booking area and procedures and sleeping on the floor in the holding tank with 25 to 30 other men, I counted it as a joy. Freedom was on the way and nothing would steal my joy.

After laying on that floor for about four days I was taken to a section called WX two days before my hearing. In my mind, I was prepared for everything until the morning of the hearing when my nerves reminded me to let Professor Watson do the work while I just listened.

I was not surprised to see my faithful supporters and favorite law team as I entered the courtroom. We were all hopeful.

Our first witness would be a doctor who held a Ph. D. in genetics and was the current lab chief at Cell mark. I wasn't sure what he would say but from what I had read it would be more trouble for the state lab.

Q. As to the serology inclusions of exhibit 56 (the chart) in the face of DNA exclusions that existed at the time as to the mixture of semen stains what is your opinion?

A. When you have six or seven alleles that take into

account more people in the population and if I found that the suspect could not be excluded from that mixture, which is obviously a large mixture of many people and I say he can't be excluded and the statistics for his profile is found in one in forty quadrillion Caucasian individuals, let's say for an example. That would be very misleading. Because the only thing you can really report is the chance of anyone being in that mixture is one in fifty, not that his profile is one in forty quadrillion because that's completely meaningless in that case.

The judge sought clarification regarding exhibit 56 and the following exchange occurred by the court: so let's look at line 8C on this chart, there's a 64 next to that line, but that refers to Roosevelt Glenn.

A. Okay.

Court: So we have his standard.

A. Right.

Court: It says that particular standard is going to occur in every four people in the general population, and three point seven five (3.75) out of 100 of the black population.

A. Yes.

Court: is there anything misleading in that?

A. I think it's very misleading.

Court: Explain to me why.

A. Because that is totally, totally irrelevant piece of information until you match him to a specimen that only comes from one individual that completely matches him.

Court: I see.

A. Alright.

Q. So if Glenn has been excluded by DNA testing as being a contributor to mixture of stain 3.1 and all other stains, a serology argument that would include in it, would you agree that's false?

A. I would have a very hard time believing it, yes. What I would believe is that it's just a serendipitous thing, that there's a high probability of matching so he does, whereas the DNA testing, the chance of falsely matching is incredibly low and, therefore, he's excluded.

The judge, I believe had the most important single exchange in the entire hearing, when the court asked, "Doctor, in a nutshell, none of the fluids or hair tested was contributed by Roosevelt Glenn?"

A. That is correct.

Judge: You may step down.

I don't know if I was tripping or not, but it looked like the judge was looking straight at me throughout the witnesses' testimony. Then it was as though a light finally went on in his head and he could now see everything clearly.

Although I still was not allowed to say anything to anyone, I wanted to say so much but I settled for the conversation in my head. "Judge, we don't need to go any further, do we? I now know we don't for sure, because I can see it in your face. We both know this is a rape case and the semen on the vaginal swab is not mine, and the semen in the stain labeled 3.1, 3.2, 3.3, 3.4, is not mine. Oh yea, by the way, the head hair that they say matched 26 characteristics of mine and was unlikely to come from anyone else because of those unique characteristics, has been proven by DNA testing not to be mine. What more could you possibly want, to prove I didn't rape this victim. Oh and one more thing judge that pubic hair combed out of her private area has also been tested and proven not to be mine, and don't forget my two co-defendants have also been excluded from everything. Damn, what else do you need to prove my innocence? I've taken every test science has to offer and passed each one. So, you can go ahead and do the right thing everyone would understand if you stop this nonsense from continuing."

I came back to my attorney addressing the fact that her next two witnesses were the prosecutors who tried this case back in 1993. They were both in the courtroom. One of them has been co-counsel throughout this hearing for the state. Of course they gave an objection saying it was not necessary or proper for a defendant to question a prosecutor. The judge agreed and denied our motion and subpoena to question the prosecutors, even though they were there and allowed to sit in the courtroom.

My attorney began to argue to the court that her line of questioning of the prosecutors would be limited to specifically their knowledge of who made this wall size chart used against Glenn and about their knowledge of DNA testing overriding serology.

There has been testimony from witnesses that the person who created the chart knew or should have known that what she was doing was malfeasance, but there has been nothing from the state prosecutors. The state's attempt to avoid this claim is based in large part on an argument that if the state should have known that the serology evidence was false or misleading then so too should have Glenn at the time of his trial and he should have objected to it, therefore this is a procedural default. But this argument or claim misses the point of the Brady/Napue line of cases wherein the issue, for determining the willfulness of the violation, is what the state knew and when the state knew it.

Criminal defendants cannot call the trial court prosecutors as witnesses at time of trial, any evidence relating to Glenn's claim that the state offered or failed to correct false or misleading testimony relating to serology was always and necessarily going to be a beyond-the-record claim that could only realistically be presented in a post-conviction relief action, which we bring before the court now your honor.

Court: I'm satisfied that the earlier ruling was correct under these circumstances. If the evidence is as you suggest false and misleading in the way that it was presented. The state is right. The record speaks for itself, and it's not necessary to call either prosecutor to establish that.

What, what did he just say? If, the evidence is false and misleading, what hearing have you been absorbing in your brain? Have you not been paying attention to all the experts? This sounds like he's full of Bull! His decision to quash those subpoenas made me feel he was saying I wasn't good enough as a defendant to question the likes of a prosecutor he sounded as though he was offended by the thought of a defendant questioning a prosecutor even through his attorney. The way he responded was as though it was his job to protect these guys, as friends do for one another. Now I was left to wonder did he also feel it was his job to protect the state lab as well, which also got it wrong. My whole fight was these prosecutors and the state lab. Why should they be protected and not me? I didn't know what to do or think so I just stopped and let my attorney finish her work.

The judge continued: That is the ruling of this court. Are there any more witnesses from the defendant?

Professor Watson: No, your Honor the defense rests its case.

Court: And will the prosecutors be calling any witnesses?

Prosecutors: No, Your Honor.

Court: If that's all the witnesses we'll take a half hour break, conclude with final arguments and I will give my decision today. Court is now in recess.

Being taken back to this dark and cozy sewage smelling cell for the next half hour would be torture for me. All I could hear over and over again was the words motion denied. I'm very glad that this decision was only for this particular motion that would be the only positive to draw from this denial.

This is the way I've conditioned my thinking in all matters. Going back to the courtroom, I put on my positive face and positive attitude after the half hour of solitude. Everyone was still uplifted with smiles and waves as I entered the courtroom.

It crossed my mind to wonder if some of these beautiful faces and smiles were just a façade. Did my lawyer and her students look one way but feel different on the inside just to keep me encouraged? Whatever the case, we were all on one accord and the positivity soaring throughout the courtroom was amazing.

The prosecutors helped boost our confidence because they didn't call one witness to refute any of the testimony given by all the experts. So I'm thinking this is a slam-dunk with only the finishing touches in the way of closing arguments. It was time, the judge entered the courtroom and the first line of business was closing arguments.

Judge: Are you ready to precede counsel.

Professor Watson: Yes, Your Honor. In this extraordinary case your honor the prosecutor at Glenn's trial presented the completely and inaccurate and misleading testimony. And then relied upon the testimony in their closing argument. The prosecution also created and presented a poster board size chart of misleading and irrelevant serological data based on the testimony which has been subsequently characterized as being indicative of either incompetence or malfeasance. The defense attorney did not object to the serology testimony at trial. The state falsely upped the erroneous conclusions further in their closing argument. In addition, the state used a hair as associative evidence, overstating its value significantly, and that hair has now been shown to be from someone other than Glenn. Important policy considerations support requiring lawyers to research and understand the testimony presented, but Glenn's attorney and trial prosecutors didn't. Lawyers are considerably more educated than most jurors. If the lawyer does not understand the testimony and/or presents it inaccurately, most jurors will not give the scientific testimony its proper weight. The verdict is not based on truth or facts, but on lay jurors' impressions and gut reactions after hours of complicated scientific testimony. Without a doubt, false scientific testimony in the form of microscopic hair comparison and serology inclusions were presented at Glenn's trial. Whether the fault lies with the prosecution or the scientific results in which such testimony is presented does not comport with the requirement of fundamental fairness. When no identification was made of Glenn, the defense alibi was corroborated, and informants accounted for the strength of the state's case. The prosecutors' false summary in closing arguments demonstrates the fundamental unfairness of this trial without doubt. The state blatantly mischaracterized testimony in closing argument. The jury would have assumed the prosecution was presenting meaningful scientific testimony.

The investigation and trial of Glenn's included many of the variables, which are now, associated with wrongful convictions: Junk science, jailhouse testimony, suggestive identification, and police tunnel vision. The hair was not Glenn's and the jury thought it was. The DNA was not his and the jury was told serology included Glenn in stains that included almost all person. DNA (RFLP) testing had excluded Glenn and the two men he was with that fatal night. Trial counsel did not act competently in regard to the scientific evidence. Justice is not blind. The trial and conviction is the essence of unfair. Glenn urges this court to recognize this injustice and on the unequivocal facts in this case, reverse this conviction. The mitochondria DNA testing of the hair from the victim's sweater constitutes newly discovered evidence. In addition, Roosevelt Glenn was unconstitutionally convicted with junk science, including the erroneous microscopic hair comparison and highly prejudicial, irrelevant, misleading, false, serology testimony. Glenn's attorney failed to understand the science and preserve his rights. Roosevelt Glenn is innocent and his conviction is a travesty. His petition should be granted, his conviction reverse, and a new trial order forth with. This case doesn't add up judge, and we leave it in your hands. We appreciate your time and attention.

By the court: After listening to the arguments and considering this I believe I'm prepared to proceed to ruling, before I begin to issue a formal ruling I want to thank the parties for their high level of professionalism on both sides. Obviously, a great deal of work has gone into this, and of course it goes without saying that a great many emotions are involved. I've given this a great deal of consideration. I understand that this is life or death for many people. This is Mr. Glenn's freedom, but after considering everything that's been presented I conclude that the petitioner has failed to establish that the newly discovered evidence is sufficient to exonerate Mr. Glenn, and I therefore recommend that the petition for post-conviction relief be denied. That is the judgment of the court.

Oh no, this was a repeat performance from 1993 only this time I couldn't move my body or swallow. This time was more of a shock than before because his look was one of empathy, but his decision was one of loyalty. I know I must have appeared cool and calm because I couldn't move my body but my mind was at it again.

My mind was racing, wait a minute, Judge, this forensic science bull used at trial has been shown to be invalid. Doesn't that count for anything? This DNA is newly discovered evidence that is factual, that in itself should be enough to override that circumstantial bull about green coveralls and some jailhouse snitches who got a favor for their testimonies and I'm not supposed to exonerate myself, but show that this new evidence could cause a jury

81

on retrial to have reasonable doubt or may not have convicted me had they known about this evidence. You can't be serious. I'm no lawyer, Judge, but I know I'm right about this one; you should call somebody to make sure you're applying the law properly in this case. I mean, come on, you're going to destroy my mom, hurry up and correct yourself before she hears you. I gave myself a pinch, it was then I heard the cry of my mom above all else. I turned to her with my look of confidence and saw her and my sister locked together not knowing who was holding who, my ex-wife with water rolling down her face trying to hold back the tears, my children with tears of anger and disappointment and the sounds of disbelief throughout the courtroom. The law students were in tears and my attorney was fighting back the tears trying to stay professional, but a look of shock on her face.

The judge stormed out of the courtroom. It was then the students came toward me, as I finally stood to my feet to meet them. They all began to hug me and the professor. That's when something inside me took over and I assured them that I was ok. I told them, remember my words I'm prepared for whatever comes my way and whatever doesn't. So cheer up, the fight is not over I need you all to be all right to help me continue this fight and not give up. Okay. I looked them all in their eyes as I spoke. I turned to my family and friends to shout, don't worry I'm coming home November 2009 anyway. I made eye contact with my children, ex-wife, mom, sister, and brother. Just get ready for our celebration, November 2009! No one can stop that date from happening. Hold on to that as your encouragement, I told them all I loved them and thanks for everybody coming out as I was being escorted out the courtroom. I could still see and hear the pain and disappointment of everyone in the courtroom even the different reporters were still there looking confused.

On the way back to my section, the man escorting me

was saying, "Man I don't know how you do it, I would be mad as hell, are you really okay?" I do it because I've been keeping my faith no matter what things look like or feel like. I still believe a blessing is on the way.

When I got back to my section in the county jail, everybody was asking what's up Old School. Everybody has been pulling for you, come on man what happened.

"I was denied", I said. I was shocked to guys getting angry for me, asking me if I needed anything. One guy said if anybody had a chance it was you, now it looks like nobody can win in this county even if you didn't do it. Guys began to say I know you're mad now, Old School. I was when I first heard the judges' decision but only for a little while, as I am human. Then I had to reach down deep inside myself and use what God had given me – strength to be an overcomer.

The Bible tells us to be angry, but sin not. It's all about what you do with that anger. I choose to turn it into something positive, anything positive out of this negative situation.

I was able to show a right attitude and righteous living in the midst of a real storm. The guys respected me for my reaction to this hard pill to swallow.

Final Return

On the way back to prison, even the transport officers said they didn't think I'd be going back to prison. They made my trip back as comfortable as possible and they talked to me for almost the entire three-hour ride back. They were telling me about all the different type of telephones, computers and how they functioned. They told me about the struggles people were having with the economy and advised me not to rush to catch up on everything when I got out. They told me to take whatever job I could get and whatever assistance was available for me. Bottom line was don't be too proud to ask for or accept help.

I knew it wasn't going to be easy going back into society at 47 years old and trying to start life over from scratch, but I was as ready as anyone could be.

Just like I first believed God would send someone to help expose this injustice, I now had to believe that someone would be placed in a position to act appropriately with the law and reverse this travesty of justice.

Coming back to MCF was going to be a surprise to everyone who knew my situation because no one was expecting me to return. I had even given some of my things away that would have to be returned should I come back. It was a part of our agreement and giving our word was all we had to validate our character.

I was assigned to the same building when I returned but on the opposite side. Everyone looked like they had seen a ghost when they saw me. Some of the guys were saying, no way, come on man. Tell us you're waiting for a decision.

"No", I said, "this is the decision. The judge shot me down". This went on for about a week as guys would see me and just shake their heads in disbelief that I was still there. I did get my items back, some things I didn't care to have back and gave it as a gift but I had to inquire about everything, as though they were my items, because if I didn't it would be a sign of weakness instead of kindness.

As the days and weeks went by all was back to normal and it was time for school. This would be my final semester to assure my November 2009 release date. I had everybody looking for my release date to be in 2009 instead of the original 2011 date.

I focused on school as much as possible. My classes were more intense than I expected. I had a full load of six classes, which kept my mind away from all the court stuff. My first two months was going well, my lowest grade had only been a B+, so I was really into my schooling.

Then came October and things began to get a little more complicated. The case was getting close to being filed in the Indiana Court of Appeals and to complicate things my counselor told me I was on the list to be transferred again.

D.O.C. has now decided to house those labeled as sex offenders at the New Castle Facility. They have the better Facility for the therapeutic treatment being used on sex offenders that has now become mandatory. This facility had the necessary rooms to accommodate more group sessions at a time.

New Castle became available after Indiana had failed in its efforts to house prisoners by contract from Arizona. These inmates became very hostile after being transferred to Indiana, which had a lot more restrictions on inmates than they were lead to believe. The Arizona prisoners attempted a takeover by holding staff members inside buildings and setting fires. Some staff members were hurt as well as some inmates but there were no reported deaths. After all this, the Arizona inmates were relocated back to Arizona and it left one half the prison empty with the other side of the prison filled with Indiana inmates.

It was immediately available for 1,050 inmates. After hearing the news, I just wondered how I was going to finish college. I only had 1½ months to go. If I didn't complete this semester I would have to start all over with my fourth semester being at New Castle, which wouldn't start until January. I was doing so well in school that I definitely didn't want to start over.

I made a request to stay until I finished school. The counselor told me that the decision was out of her control. As I went back to my cell, I just prayed about it. The worst case would be to repeat the semester and hopefully my grades would not be hurt so I could finish in December 2008 or May 2009 and still be able to get out in November 2009.

December 2008 graduation ceremony from Ball State University with an Associate of Arts Degree attended by my mom and sister at New Castle, Indiana.

Court of Appeals

A couple of weeks went by and finally some good news came by way of a visit from the law students. The case had been filed in the Indiana Court of Appeals on October 27, 2008. They were excited and I was overjoyed as they went over the actual brief filed by the Professor. Everything sounded so promising. In the process I had become a student of the law and now I understand a lot more than I did before. We laughed and talked about some of their future employment and challenges facing them, hoping we could all have a big celebration before my November 2009 release.

When the visit was over I went back and began to read the brief again and again. It was so inspiring I couldn't get enough of it. It was everything I hoped for. No one could have done better work in my opinion. I couldn't sleep and before I knew it, it was time for school

I was so tired and the day couldn't end quickly enough. During class I was not absorbing anything, while taking notes but after class I was told that the counselor wanted to see me. It was nerve-racking because I was afraid it was my time to prepare for transfer out. She must have seen my worry on my face because her first words were to relax. She told me that I would get to finish the semester here, at MCF but that after college I would be one of the first to be transferred.

The delay was good news. I called everyone including my attorney. I finished school as planned in December 2008 and was transferred to my 5th prison a week later. This transfer was a lot smoother than the last one because the non-sex offenders were not housed in the same area. The non-sex offenders were divided by way of a fence because of some of the beatings and abuse. I would have preferred not to be separated because I knew most of the men on the other side of that fence but for a majority of people it was best for their own protection. I also knew that this separation would cause a lack of movement on our side of the fences meaning less job opportunity, programs, recreation, which ended up being true.

Even though there were two sides of the fence, we couldn't mingle in offender population, which put a serious hold on the south side because the north side was already established in all the main buildings. This lack of movement went on for several months, which became very frustrating to everyone. Then a memo went out to the north side that they would be losing some jobs and most would be moving out soon. The plans were to make the entire camp for sex offenders. The north side began to move out twice a week. Things began to open up on the south side of the fence, as this side became the majority.

During this time my attorney filed paperwork that made me exempt from participation in the therapeutic classes we were sent to attend. The main office granted my exemption because my case was re-opened and on appeal with my rights being renewed to maintain my innocence. This was very important because in the classes you were to admit your guilt and explain why you committed the crime. If not, you would be sanctioned with more possible time.

This requirement got my attorney involved, because I

could not and would not admit to something I didn't do.

On January 30, 2009, the attorney general filed his brief in the Indiana Court of Appeals in support of the decision made by Lake County to continue pursuing a denial of my conviction being overturned.

The Attorney General of Indiana agreed with the finding of Lake County as it related to the jailhouse testimony, the green coveralls left with the victim, and the identification of a co-defendant.

So much was made about the identification of my co-defendant which was used against me at my trial. And at his trial so much was made about this head hair identified as belonging to me which was used against him at his trial. We both had different jailhouse snitches testifying in each of our trials. But in the end no one identified me and no evidence ever identified me. Ever.

And there was more to this travesty. First, my co-defendant being identified was bogus and here's why: The victim says consistently that she could not identify any of the men who had attacked her. She never viewed a physical line up and never viewed a photographic array of the suspects. However, sometime in January 1990, the lead investigator took the mug shots of the defendants to the victims' home to show them to her. He set these photographs on the dining room table where the victim, and her husband were seated. The victim stated that he did not ask her to look at the pictures.

Come on. Why would he take pictures to the victim's house and not ask her to look at them? I believe this is where they were getting confused on what to say. I believe that the victim was being coerced into identifying somebody. In reading the transcripts of the exchange between the detective and the Professor.

As she questioned him about these photos:

Q: Detective, did you offer to show these pictures to her?

A: Yes.

Q: And Glenn's picture was on top?

A: Yes

Q: Why not do a physical line up?

A: She said she couldn't identify anybody.

Q. So, then why take the pictures to show them to her?

A: They had threatened her family if they went to police. We live in a multi-racial area. She said she couldn't identify anybody, we arrested the people we suspected of committing this crime, and so I was going to let them look at these people so they could protect themselves, if they're confronted by any of them on the street.

Q. But wouldn't you agree that might compromise her future identification, when she could not make one.

A. It wasn't going to be identification at that point, as far as I was concerned. But in May 1990 the victim attended a pretrial conference knowing that the co-defendant would be there and made the only identification in this case. While he was in court the following was asked of the victim.

Q. Did there come a time during the morning court call that the co-defendant's case was called here at the lectern before the bench?

A. Yes.

Q. And did he identify himself?

A. Yes.

Q. And was he in court with his counsel?

A. Yes, he was.

Professor Watson then states to the court, for the record: Given the circumstances of the identification of the co-defendant and the use of this identification against Glenn, the case of the United States Vs. Telfaire 469F2d552, is being offered as evidence in Glenn's post-conviction action as it is considered a landmark case on the factors which make an identification suggestive (invalid).

If these types of identifications are factual evidence trumping DNA evidence in Indiana's courts of law then why do states pay for DNA testing?

The victim says she can't identify her attackers while under oath and so does the lead detective. But after the mug shot incidents she can now do an in-court ID when she knew he would be appearing in court. They were so sure she couldn't ID anyone they never had a standard line up physical or photo.

Then there are the jailhouse snitches that were also a crucial tool to the prosecutors' case according to the court's decision in denying my appeal for freedom. Even after the Professor's research on this matter. She revealed that false jailhouse testimony is now recognized as one of the leading causes of wrongful convictions in the United States. A study of the (111) persons exonerated after being on death row found false jailhouse testimony was present in 45% of those cases. A revelation made by Northwestern University School of law Center on wrongful convictions, the snitch system, P.3 (2005). Indiana has recognized that the credibility of a felon witness is highly suspect.

State vs. Bowen's 722 N.E. 2nd 368, 369 (Ind. Ct. App. 2000). An investigation undertaken in Los Angeles County, California is instructive on this point. The report of the 1989-90 Los Angeles County Grand Jury Investigation of jailhouse snitches in the criminal justice system is the most comprehensive study of jailhouse informants to date. The report concluded that there had been an appalling number of instances of perjury or other falsifications to law enforcement during the past ten years. The grand jury found that informants, in order to fabricate confessions, actively sought information from arrest reports, newspapers, and from friends and family outside of the jail. These informants did not feel constrained by external or internal values to refrain from lying, regardless of the consequences to other inmates. The United States

Court of Appeals for the ninth circuit has also recognized the danger of jailhouse informant testimony in 2001. The court stated: never has it been more true than it is now that a criminal charged with a serious crime understands that a fast and easy way out of trouble with the law is not only to have the best lawyer money can buy or the court can appoint, but to cut a deal at someone else's expense and to purchase leniency from the government by offering testimony in return for immunity or in return for reduced incarceration. In response to what these jurisdictions have discovered, the American Bar Association passed resolution addressing jailhouse informant testimony, which states: Resolved, that the American Bar Association urges federal, state, local, and territorial governments to reduce the risk of convicting the innocent, while increasing the likelihood of convicting the guilty by ensuring that no prosecution should occur based solely upon uncorroborated jailhouse informant testimony. Resolution 1086 of the American Bar Association House of Delegates, February 14, 2005.

Concluding her research, Professor Watson went on to show how the jailhouse snitches in this case should fail by stating: The testimony of the jailhouse informants in Glenn's' trial is highly problematic for several reasons. The Lead detective cast a wide net for informants, bringing men down from their jail cells in groups of more than five men, this is an extremely ill-advised tactic. Studies have documented that convicts will seek information in order to create fraudulent confessions in exchange for leniency. Here in, law enforcement actively sought the assistance of jailhouse informants, opening the door to the distinct possibility of perjury.

The informant in Glenn's trial, testified that Glenn and an unknown number of his friends: went riding and looking for a girl to rob, Glenn said they ran into the back of a car, he didn't say who was driving or nothing, he said they got out and the lady got out to see if there was any damages. His friends got out of the car and they grabbed her.

The informant in the co-defendant's trial testified that the two co-workers were drinking outside of the liquor store when two more fellows that work with them had pulled up in this car with a woman in the back seat with coveralls over her head.

The professor went on to say, "Obviously, beyond their inconsistencies with each other signaling that one or the other is untrue, both informants versions conflict with the victims account of the event. The victim stated that at the time she was abducted all five assailants were present. She also stated that each of the five raped her and all five ejaculated."

The story of two men pulling up with a woman in the back seat cannot be reconciled with the victim's statements. He also testified that one of the defendants did not ejaculate. But more importantly for the Glenn sufficiency issues, the depiction of the rape is also directly conflict with the victim's facts.

One informant stated that Glenn tried to stop them after he saw what they were doing to her. He also said that Glenn did not rape the victim, but that he kissed her. The victim did not testify that any of her assailants only kissed her or tried to help her.

She continues to discredit the use of these two informants testimony by stating that the testimony of the informants is striking in its similarity – the versions became more detailed with time. Both were interviewed shortly after the defendants had been released pretrial.

At the time, both men gave substantially less detailed stories than those later testified to at trial. One of the men, in the initial interview, discussed Glenn dropping people off and he even mentioned that Glenn's green coveralls had been stolen. At that time, he did not mention anything about a rape. It was not until November 22, 1991 that he gave his account featuring the rape, including specific street names. At this time, he was in prison, having been convicted of a new auto theft case. The record of the statement given November 22, 1991 is hand written by the detective with the informant's signature. This hand written statement was shown to the informant before he testified. As set forth in further detail in the statement of the facts, particularly in light of its conflict with the victim's testimony and the fact that he changed his report of the details of this supposed confession a year and a half after he had been incarcerated with Glenn, the informant testimony should fail or be given very little weight.

Listening to the professor talk about the testimony of these two informants and my co-defendant being identified in the courtroom made me wish that I could have had her for my actual trial back in 1993. There was no way a jury of my peers would have convicted me with the evidence being explained and challenged like the professor was doing. She made it so clear and understandable for the average person.

All the physical evidence no longer links me to this crime, by way of DNA testing. And the circumstantial evidence was a reasonable doubt.

Even going back to the night in question when the car was stranded on the highway she brought out that as we walked away from the vehicle and talked with the state trooper there was no mention of anyone of us carrying the duffle bags or green coveralls that we all testified were left in the car and were eventually stolen by highway bandits that committed this crime that I'm serving the time for.

The one question that the detective never answered was how the three of us get the green 4-door Catalina used in this crime that belongs to a man who testified he didn't know me or loan me his car.

According to the prosecutor's theory at trial, after cashing our paychecks at 12:25 a.m., we connected with two unidentified men and got into the car without the owner present. The car was identified by combining an attempted victim's description of the vehicle that bumped her car with the actual victim's description of her assailants' car. The detective concluded that the car was used in the attacks. The detective first became aware of the vehicle after speaking to an employee at the steel mill. The car belonged to a man who worked with the janitorial service at the steel mill.

The detective inquired about a mid-70's green GM car with circular, side-by-side headlights, and he discovered a vehicle matching that description. His description included the fact that both women described the car being very dirty. He determined that this car was the only car registered in Lake and Porter counties that fit the description of the one used in the attacks. He concluded that the only vehicle fitting the description would be the 1973 Pontiac Catalina. He then determined that there were only 231,973 Catalina's' registered in Lake county and Porter County. Specifically, he stated that this car was the only car that was being driven to the steel mill that fit all the characteristics that both women ultimately identified.

This circumstantial evidence was not even in the court ruling and no emphasis was added to this car situation. Why? I would guess because no witness could testify that we were in this vehicle on the night in question. As a matter of fact the car we rode in coming from work was a red Ford Escort. The car we were picked up in on that night was a powder or light blue two-door with a bright white top.

No green car was ever in our possession and that's why the detective would rather have this car forgotten. You would think this green car would be talked about because it was the tool used for this crime and possibly others. My trial attorney back in 1993 did not trust the detective and now we know that her instincts were right.

The detective has since been exposed for using illegal tactics. Another guy in our county was freed from prison after twenty years because DNA testing proved that he was wrongfully convicted back in 1981 and the lead detective in his case was this detective who is now listed in a multimillion-dollar lawsuit because of this case.

The newspaper reported about a lawsuit against the city of Hammond, it became a re-casting of a 1981 trial that ended with the defendant's wrongful conviction. The attorney, who prosecuted the case in 1981, testified he was not aware that the victim underwent an hour-long hypnosis session with police detectives before she identified the defendant as one of her two attackers.

I'm not saying that my co-defendants identification in the case I'm fighting was through hypnosis, but I will say it was strange that the victim couldn't identify any of her attackers until the same detective showed up at her house with photos of us.

In the *Post Tribune* article, the Prosecutor stated that while acknowledging other factors would have played into his decision, the 1981 case might never have made it to trial if he had known about the hypnosis session and other questionable practices used by Hammond detectives.

An attorney in the case asked the prosecutor, "In your mind, there is a real question as to whether you would've even been able to go to trial?" The original prosecutor answered, "Yes and this defendant is seeking millions in damage from the city and the detective who supervised the departments' detectives during the 1980's."

He claimed that the trial and his wrongful imprisonment, violated his civil rights. This trial continued with his former attorney, Professor Watson, from the Indiana University Law Clinic, who worked with law students to win his release.

Professor Watson was an angel sent from heaven. She was able to prove his wrongful conviction and now she is fighting hard to prove my innocence as well as co-defendant. What are the odds that she would get two cases in the same county years apart with the same lead detective?

That defendant won his civil suit, the newspaper reported that he said if he had to choose, he'd rather have the years of his lost freedom back. But since those years were long gone, he was very happy with the money the jury awarded him. He was awarded $500,000 for each year he was in prison for a 1980 rape he didn't commit bringing the total to around $9 million.

"The city and the detective would have to come up with the money", His attorneys said, "and we would also ask for an additional $1 million for attorney fees." Attorneys for the city and for the detective left the courtroom immediately. "It was justice for the city and detective who treated him no better than an animal, during their original investigation, trial, and ensuing prison time. The city of Hammond should take this as a wakeup call."

I believed that this evidence should affect the

credibility of that same detective who led the investigation into my case during the same period of time (1980s). Law enforcement should be held accountable for any type of bad ethics when it is revealed.

We all know when something like this occurs, it is not the first time. Bad ethics usually have a pattern that could extend over many years. My case was one of his biggest cases and he desperately wanted to crack the case.

No one could ever convince me that he ran this case by the book, because if he had I wouldn't be writing this book from behind prison walls. And now that the other case has been exposed to the public it only strengthens my belief.

The sad part about this exposure is that we know he didn't act alone. The prosecutor also stated that there were other questionable practices used by the detectives. I am sure that the county court denying my appeal was part of a ploy to protect the detective, the prosecutors and the state laboratory.

But now, it will only be a matter of time before the Court will expose them and this injustice after completing a review on the incompetence of the evidence being used to uphold this conviction.

I'm sure it's hard to openly admit when a mistake has been made of this magnitude. I realized early on that I have to continue my journey by faith and not allow my thoughts to be corrupted by my experiences or my environment, especially when around new staff members at the new location.

All it would take is one person to say that I could not adjust to the new environment and I would probably be requested to seek psychological treatment. It never happened before and I wanted to keep it that way.

That's why after being exempt from the SOMM (Sex

Offender Management and Monitoring) Program, I applied for everything dealing with education and self-help programs. My first choice was substance abuse. Substance abuse has a two-fold purpose for me. One would be self-help and the other would be a 3 to 6 month time cut depending on how far I went through the program.

Inmates who completed 4 months successfully would receive 90-days cut off their sentence. It was important to me to do all I could to help myself. I would find myself stopping by the counselor's office everyday inquiring about my substance abuse application and making sure I was up front during mail call in case the answer came by mail.

It literally took 60 days and on the 60th day I received my application with the red stamp "Denied". I stood there and read this denial as though someone was lying or playing a joke. I looked around to see if someone was watching for my response to maybe laugh at something or me. But nobody looked my way.

I was about to yell out in disappointment but as I read down the page further it stated my score was too high. Now I know something is wrong because you can't score too high to receive treatment. That's unheard of so somebody just blew the game with that comment.

Then I smiled and realized that it didn't matter that no one was looking my way because I knew this was not real. But damn this is my handwriting. Who could possible imitate my handwriting this perfectly? Now, I'm tripping, this got to be real it's my writing. How can they say my score is too high?

Early the next morning I was up pacing the floors waiting for the counselor to show up for work. I wanted to be the first person on the list to see the counselor. When the officer came and called my name I couldn't get out the door quick enough hoping the counselor would tell me there was a typing error on my paper work and that I could attend substance abuse treatment classes.

After saying our good mornings, I got straight to the point. I said, "I need you to look at my application for substance abuse because I believe someone made a mistake." He looked over the application and said, "You scored too high, but that's the first time I've gotten one like this." He told me to wait while he made a quick call.

After the phone call he looked at me while hanging up the phone and said, "I'm sorry Glenn, but they say we are not equipped with the type of treatment you need at this facility. You need more of a therapeutic community type treatment, which we have yet to acquire at this prison. Your need is more intense than we can provide at this time. "

I went back to my bunk disappointed which was normal for me. All I could do was laugh, and smile, to keep from crying.

But I didn't realize my outward expression was so obvious. Some of the guys were asking, "What's the good news Glenn?" I replied, "I just got denied from substance abuse because I scored too high on my application. So I don't qualify for treatment or the 3 to 6 month possible time cut." Everyone who heard my response began to shout, "Glenn, you can't score too high for treatment." I laid the paperwork down on the table and kept walking. I could hear the guys read my denial and say that's bull, no one ever heard of that before.

Sitting on my bunk, I began to fill out a request for interview form. On this request I stated that I had been in prison for the last 16 years without any type of drug or alcohol use and with 16 years of clean random urinalysis testing.

One of the main reasons for applying to this program was for preventive measures. After 16 years I would be re-entering society faced with all kinds of obstacles and unknowns. My goal was to leave this facility with all the tools I could possibly obtain to prepare myself for what I was about to face. Any kind of substance abuse training available could, without a doubt, assist me in making a successful transition. This program was the last tool I needed to equip myself to be the best that I could be. Thank you for your time and consideration.

Filling out this request made me feel good about doing all I could to help myself. All I could do was wait for a response still hoping for the best.

Another 29 days went by and on the 30th day I received several pieces of interdepartmental mail. One was my request for interview form sent to substance abuse stamped "denied".

But this time the response was for a totally different reason. The form stated, "Mr. Glenn, you do not qualify for substance abuse as you do not have the required amount of time left on your sentence."

While shaking my head in disbelief, I hurried to open the remaining mail. It was unanimous, all my mail was stamped denied. I didn't qualify for any programs. That included computers, master student and horticulture. My biggest fear had just surfaced. The college time cut I got for obtaining an associate's degree was now posted on the statewide computer system. This was my reason for applying for everything as quickly as possible, because I had a grace period to get into any programs available to me that my amount of time left would allow.

At this facility you had to have 15 months or more to

qualify for programs. I now only had 9 months left on my sentence. Other prisons only wanted you to have enough time on your sentence to complete the program. For example, I had 9 months left to do and substance abuse could be completed in 4 months and you get a 3 month time cut which would be just enough time at other camps but at this camp, you couldn't even apply unless you had 15 months or more, which will someday change now that people are being transferred to this prison with shorter time but not now and not for me.

But right now I'm going to have to suffer the consequences of the decisions made and the policies in place. It's almost as though they were waiting for my grace period to expire before responding to any of my requests.

But I keep moving forward on my next option to apply for a job. I've kept myself busy the entire time I've been locked up. Being without work, school, or programs will make time really slow. My job search didn't take long. I was offered a job in the dorm I was living in. I started working immediately cleaning whatever needed to be cleaned particularly bathrooms, windows, and microwaves. I bet we had the cleanest in the prison, I would clean all day long even when my hours were over for the day, if my areas looked unclean I wouldn't hesitate to clean them. I did this for days until one day I decided to make sure I was on the payroll, because I never received any confirmation. I was only verbally told I was on the payroll.

When I checked the counselor told me there was no record of me having a job. The paper work must have been misplaced somewhere so I was working for free. You're telling me I've been busting my butt for about four weeks and won't get any pay? That's right.

Again I left his office politely and headed back to my bunk, which had become my safe haven, and my place for solitude. At this point I would not move another muscle to work. I didn't care how nasty this place got I'd just clean when I need to use certain areas.

This prison would now become different than all the other ones. I had so much time on my hands observing my surroundings became automatic.

What I mean is that I noticed everything that I was blind to before. Ever since DOC started segregation in the prison system in 2006, it became a nightmare for me. I was being housed with the most looked down upon prisoners in all the prisons in the country.

I always thought that anyone who hurts a child or has to take sex from a woman is someone I would have no choice but to despise. At one time in my life I would have wanted to execute that person myself. So I felt that in order for me to make this journey successful keeping a blind eye to my surroundings would be key. It started out as the most difficult time of this bit. I always wanted to react every time someone would point out a child molester. It always felt like my duty to beat his brains out an even though the rapist was the one pointing out the child molester. I could easily break off a piece of iron in his gut as well.

The thoughts came and I had to work hard not to entertain them. This fight with my conscience went on for the first year, which took a lot of prayer and wisdom to overcome. Now that I'm bored with this idleness the characteristics of some inmates around me are being magnified.

For instance, the guy who sleeps above me has those traditional state issued thick lens glasses, and he always walks around looking at people licking his lips and smiling joyfully when kid shows are on TV. His demeanor was very annoying to me. I remember one time asking him a question and he couldn't give me an answer because it seemed as though he was so excited from me talking to him he just stuttered, smiled, and licked his lips. It didn't help knowing this guy had multiple child molesting cases.

Meeting this guy came through another move, yes another move. This time it was only a move from "I" building to "K" building. The institution decided they wanted everyone less than 9 months to be housed in K-dorm, which holds about 210 people. I automatically qualified when my college time cut was posted state wide on the computer system.

Being around these guys would be my final test of will power, with my bunkie being my biggest test. All of these men were on their way home and would be taking with them their ways of thinking, whether good or bad. I got to witness firsthand the habits and behaviors of these men heading back to their communities. This was scary to me because all I could see was an unpleasant sight. This idle mind of mine was working overtime and I noticed everything.

When an officer would come in the dorm to ask a question or make a legitimate announcement, some guys would disrupt them with silly remarks or loud sound effects to drown out whatever the officer was trying to tell us. I mean it was worse than you would expect from a group of adult men.

I began to see that a lot of these guys were children in their minds and they didn't even realize it. Some of the men even thought it was okay to have sex with underage children. I'm pretty sure it was because, in my opinion, they couldn't deal with adulthood or adult women.

One day, I heard a guy say that he wasn't a bad person and it wasn't a big deal that he loves kids. I was so angry that I must have had a spiritual heart attack or an out of body experience because I went out of my mind and said some things I thought I would never let come out of my mouth.

I'd heard things similar to this before, but then my blind eye was in effect and my mind wasn't an idle one. The saying an idle mind is the devils workshop is true if you allow it. I just could not allow the enemy, the devil to dictate my attitude, behavior, or thoughts. I said to my negative thoughts, "devil you are a lie and the truth isn't in you". I rebuked all negative thoughts entering my mind with an immediate response to all the turmoil and insanity I was facing.

I realized I had to continue to stand on the good core values that we are all born with and to try hard to be an example for those who have lost their way and to really watch my reactions. Maybe I'll only reach one person to make a difference in his life but that would be enough.

I also found myself surrounded by guys who either worshipped the devil, practiced witchcraft or didn't believe in a God, goodness or righteousness.

My hope was to be seen as a righteous doer and not just a talker. There are a lot of men who felt comfortable talking about their crimes to me because they figured I was in for a similar crime, but what they forgot was that I plead not guilty and maintained my innocence and was still actively fighting the conviction with less than 7 months left with the hope of clearing my name totally.

I was still known as a guy who prayed a lot and I believed one of my prayers had come to pass. An officer and two case managers approached me at different times to offer me a job. This was a surprise because I had not applied or requested the particular job. This job offer would give me the chance to be out of the dorm for 5 hours a day 7 days a week. The pay would be 15 cents an hour or 75 cents a day. Yes, were the words out of my mouth, I couldn't say no. Besides it was rare for both case managers and the officers to agree on one person. I was so ready to change from being idle so I started work as soon as possible. The new job was going very well and I kept busy all day every day.

Devastated

One morning around 11:00 a.m. an officer called my name to come pick up a call-out pass while she was standing in the doorway of the dorm I was housed in. The pass was for an attorney visit at 1:00 p.m. today's date was 4/27/09.

I wondered if the visit was from the law students with news from the court or if it was just a more casual visit to sit and talk. Did they just feel an urge to see me? Could this be the professor? She wouldn't be coming unless there was news from the court, would she? I usually got something in mail before any of them came to visit. But maybe they heard something and wanted to surprise me with some long awaited good news.

Man, I couldn't wait; this is the moment I'd been waiting for. I knew there was no way the court couldn't see through the smoke screen sent up by my county. Finally, they would have to answer for the misconduct and false testimony that put me in this place for over 16 years. Finally but right now I had to settle down because it was lunch time and I needed to eat and to breath.

I wanted to change clothes too just in case we wanted to take some pictures to capture this moment.

After eating lunch and getting prepared for the visit, I was ready for the good news that I knew had to be

107

coming from this visit.

On my way I couldn't stop the thoughts of joy and hugs I would finally get to experience. I couldn't' wait to see the smile on the professor's face after all her hard work and the hard work of the students. We would all get to smile and exhale today.

I didn't mind waiting and couldn't stop my mind from wandering through all the good thoughts a man could have at a time of victory such as this. It was a beautiful feeling.

At the door, I was able to see through the glass to the professor standing alone, which was not a good sign except maybe she wanted to be the one who brought the good news.

There would be plenty of time for celebrating and besides, I wasn't free just yet. There would be paperwork and a court appearance before my release. Her favorite words were "one step at a time". So I'll just put the celebration on ice for now and enjoy the good news and find out what the next steps would be.

As the professor got closer, I could see her through the glass and the weight on her face and body was not one of celebration. I waved with a smile but she gave no response. My God as she got closer to the window, her expression was one of sadness, and my thoughts became an "Oh no" moment, If I'm reading her correctly I need to start praying for God to intervene because this would be a hard pill for me to swallow.

Another denial might be the blow that would take me over the edge if I was going to lose it. I depended on the court to see through the truth but according to the professor they did not.

I wondered how that could be. It was clear. I was innocent. The science was the proof and I should be free. What a test. I had to decide to hold on and not allow their decision to destroy my faith and steal my joy. I needed God and my true strength more than ever. My faith had to be real rather than just talk. I had to keep myself together.

When the officer called my name he asked if I was all right because I looked like I was miles away. He tells me "good luck" as he finished the strip search. As I made my way to the visiting room, I could see the look I was afraid of through the window as I entered our private room.

She stood and greeted me with a hug of disappointment and stated we lost. She explained how she felt this court just repeated the decision of the lower court and added things that should not have been added. They can see but they just don't want to see the injustice. They ruled as though we raised a sufficiency of the evidence claim, when our claim was newly discovered evidence, and they surely didn't give the proper weight to the DNA facts.

I told her it was ridiculous, but it was not the end. We had more rounds to go so don't let this ruling weigh you down or burden you to the point you couldn't move forward, because I needed her to continue this fight. We just had to take this blow and come back even stronger. Let them know were not giving up on this fight for justice.

The court had made their ruling on April 22, 2009. The Professor told me that it was so devastating to her that it took a couple of days for her to pull herself together and bring me the news. But the students told her to come see me and she would feel better because I had that effect on people no matter how bad things seemed.

Even though her news about the case wasn't good, the vote of confidence from the students was exactly what I needed to deal with the temper tantrum in my head. I was feeling a little crazy because even though I was calm in the visiting room, I was really thinking about losing control in the dorm when I returned.

I started thinking how I wasn't gonna allow anyone to disrespect me, no one. Especially the guys who smile and lick their lips like they desire something from me. Right then, I decided I wasn't gonna fight it anymore, I was just gonna fight. No more thinking first and acting later. Someone was gonna feel my wrath today. I might as well be the beast they've labeled me to be. Yes, I'm on my way back with a smelly attitude, attack first and deal with the consequences later.

My thoughts were moving at 100 miles an hour in the wrong direction.

But I still had enough presence of mind to silently pray and ask God to give me strength he had faithfully given me for the last 16 years but make it a double portion this time because it looked like I'd be needing it. I have learned from experience that God really, really, will never leave me or forsake me. So, I called on His strength as mine has been terribly weakened.

As I silently appealed to God, the professor told me she really was feeling better after talking to me. In my mind, it was God working in and through me. God was again confirming His existence in my life even in the midst of our disappointment. We began to talk about new strategies, new hopes and an eagerness to move forward. She told me about filing a motion for transfer to the Indiana Supreme Court and about how another attorney who read the case online had contacted her with some encouraging news.

He sent her a case that had been accepted by the Supreme Court with the same issues I was fighting. This was important because the Supreme Court doesn't accept every case and this one was almost a replica of my case.

The only problem was this attorney had withdrawn

his case from the court because he received a deal for his client from the prosecutor. The case was based on newly discovered evidence. But even with that this case put the fire back into the professor's eyes and strength in her voice. We laughed and even talked about me writing a book about this experience.

We talked about barbecuing when I get out in November and how I wanted all the students to be there with my family regardless of what the court said or did. We had all become like a big extended family with plenty of love and faith to carry us through anything.

The professor told me that she thought I was a strong man and how everyone admired my positive attitude and outlook on things. She said none of us could do what you have done. Being jailed for 16 years for a crime you didn't commit and still be strong and positive and without anger throughout the entire time was to be commended

I had to tell her that it was the spirit of the God that I believe and trust in. I made it my business to always invite Him into all my situations. I told her that I did have mental battles and sometimes anger threatens to take over, but I contain the anger and negativity with righteousness. If it wasn't for people like you, the students, and my family I might be lost. So, don't think I do this by myself. You play a huge part in my life of hopes and dreams and for that I thank you.

Now, let's get past this setback and go kick some butt. The professor gave me the smile and laugh that I was hoping to see. I had regained my sense of joy.

The professor told me that she was going to also ask the court to publish this ruling so the public could see what was happening to me because the court initially ruled this decision was not for publication. She would be sending me a copy of everything she was filing on my behalf. I looked her in the eye knowing that we were getting ready to fight back with everything we had.

As I left the visiting room, the officer strip searched me again. He mentioned that I must have had good news because I wasn't acting like a person with bad news. I told him the court refused to overturn the conviction but we were going to higher courts and that my joy had to do with inviting God into the situation rather than relying on my own strength.

The officer said inviting God in is always a good thing.

As I headed back to the dorm, I thought about my initial reaction but now I was going back with a joyful spirit having conquered the giants of disappointment, anger and rage. I realized that I must have the real thing dwelling in me. Thank God.

Back at my bunk, I took a deep breath because nothing had changed around me. The same guy was licking his lips and the same guy was staring at me. I was in the same bunk in the same dorm but now I perceived it all differently. I started to see the guys as potential saints and if this is how the spirit would have me to look at these people then that's what I was gonna do. It was probably for my own good.

A few guys asked me how things went. I told them it went well even though I was denied. We were moving forward to the next court. I was blessed to have someone fighting for me.

Next I had to call everyone with the news. Mom was first as always. I broke the news gently. She thought maybe I wasn't getting released but I assured her that I was coming home but my name wouldn't be cleared and this was just another setback.

She breathed a sigh of relief and told me not to scare her like that. She just wanted me out and felt we'd work on clearing my name after my release. I told her that no one would stop my out date unless I did something stupid. I had a few more calls to make just to assure everyone that nothing, even this setback, was going to interfere with my outdate. We talked more and felt positive that the federal court would make the difference.

My last call was to my sister. She was the one that wanted to know every word that was in the decision. I had to bring the actual court decision to the phone and read it to her, even if it took two or more calls back to back to complete the reading of the decision. As I prepared myself and made the call, she answered the phone. I immediately began telling her the news. I could tell by her silence she was hurt. She wanted to know everything, so I did.

I told my sister that the courts were only going to decide the case according to the evidence most favorable to the state. The thought that any claims or arguments by us were exaggerated and frivolous even though we brought documented facts and scientific proof. The court gave our evidence no weight or consideration but I know that sooner or later they will have to acknowledge the truth so keep praying and hoping for someone to recognize the truth as its being presented.

Our conversation took two calls. We were both still stunned that even with evidence clearing me, the court still would not reverse its ruling.

We talked a little more about how things were going to be when I got home and then it was over. November was the answer and it couldn't get here fast enough.

A few days later I found myself wondering about our court system. How could my attorney be the only legal mind in the Indiana court system to see this injustice? Is it not about a person's innocence? I mean when I thought about all the science that excluded me but I was still in prison. How can there be such a divide in the system? I know first-hand what it means when we say that "We have the best legal system in the world". But best does not mean perfect because I have spent 16 years inside its imperfection and I can only hope that the percentage of wrongful convictions will lessen before being classified as an epidemic.

Now listen, if DNA is excluding the actual perpetrators of a rape, we are in trouble. This is the inference to be drawn from Indiana's court system after the rejection of my appeal, in which DNA testing excluded every suspect.

Indiana's court is saying DNA doesn't matter in the case when it favors the defendants. Everyone should beware because this is not good news for anyone who is a defendant.

I thought about the Duke Lacrosse team who had been accused of rape. Their state got it right. When DNA excluded the Lacrosse players from the crime scene they were given the benefit of the doubt as to being innocent until proven guilty. But in this case all suspects were excluded from crime scene yet three were prosecuted and two were convicted. I wondered if this was because they were from different states or simply from being black in America.

So many thoughts and questions ran through my mind after losing the trial, the direct appeal, the post-conviction relief, and now losing in Indiana's Court of Appeals. I continued to keep my head from bowing down, still spiritual, still believing in my righteous living and not letting go of hope.

Several weeks went by and my faith although shaken was as strong as ever, because over time I had learned to praise God and keep the faith in spite of my circumstances.

I received more legal mail from Professor Watson

about one month later. It was the petition to publish the court's decision to deny the appeal. The court had issued a "not for publication" decision in affirming my conviction. Professor Watson respectfully requested the court to order the publication of this entire decision.

She stated that *"the opinion in this case involves legal and factual issues of unique interest and substantial public importance to the criminal justice system in Indiana. Few published cases exist to address and clarify appropriate standards under Indiana Code in conjunction with the common law remedy of newly discovered evidence in the context of use of forensic analysis at trial now shown to be invalid. Along with this request for publication of the decision was a request for a rehearing".*

The professor was on a tear for justice. In the petition she further explained to the court why they made the wrong decision in denying my fight for a new and fair trial. She explained to the court that the hair evidence was in error and should be reconsidered.

By way of illustration, she offered the following example. Suppose there is a crime committed by a suspect identified by the victim as a white male with red hair and only one arm. The victim is certain that the perpetrator had only one arm because the perpetrator grabbed the victim's bag with one hand and hit him in the face with a stump where the other arm should have been. John Doe becomes a suspect. The victim says John Doe looks a lot like the guy who did it. However, there is a problem – John Doe has two arms neither of which has been recently transplanted onto his body. Now, John Doe belongs to some the same groups as the perpetrator: white, male, red hair. For the state to proceed to prosecute John Doe would be absurd – he could not possibly have done it.

The fact that John Doe is a white male with red hair becomes completely irrelevant in light of the fact he has both of his arms. If the victim was not certain that the perpetrator had only one arm, John Doe might look like a pretty good suspect. Given that he has both of his arms, it is impossible that John Doe was the guy who did it.

In this case, the serology evidence is like the white male with red hair facts. The DNA is like that second arm. If the serology evidence was all there was, it would be possible that Glenn could have contributed to the stains. Given the DNA evidence, it is impossible that Glenn contributed to the stains any evidence to the contrary had no place coming into Glenn's trial. That the state proffered such evidence is contrary to its duty not to put false or misleading evidence in front of the jury.

In a case prior to this one, the Supreme Court affirmed a grant of post-conviction relief on newly discovered evidence where the only omitted evidence was a recantation of prior testimony. Here, the omitted evidence is the DNA hair exclusion and the DNA exclusion from stain 3.2. Additionally, Glenn contends that at retrial, the serology evidence would be inadmissible. Given this, the fact that the state would have no scientific evidence placing Glenn at the crime scene, a jury on retrial could have a reasonable doubt as to whether the remaining circumstantial evidence was sufficient to convict.

I was not going to get to worked up over this very encouraging brief the professor has filed, even though it sounded like any blind justice should be able to see these facts as clear as day. The only problem was that getting a rehearing was almost unheard of.

It was as though I was asking a court to once again correct their own screw-up.

In my opinion and experience ... unethical.

But I'm always hopeful. As you can see by now Indiana's lab experts, in my opinion, have disgraced the state's lab. What is the protocol for the lab? Who determines if the evidence is properly analyzed and ready to be given to a court of law as fact? Who is the supervisor that signs their name confirming these results?

Labs must be held accountable for their unethical behavior when it appears. If prosecutors rely on these results to help make their case, then they too should be held accountable for not educating themselves or investigating the evidence they put before a jury.

I remember reading two books dealing with ethics, one was *Criminal Justice Today* and the other was *Ethics in the 21st Century*. Both books stated that "many people are affected by the system, whether positive or negative, the system works for some, but it also does not provide justice for others. Either way, the American criminal justice system was formed to provide social order for the people and the elements within the systems are broadened or more specified to even the playing field. The system is by no means perfect, but overall, it is effective in its quest to maintain social order as well as upholding the norm of society. The use of ethics is an important tool in justice for the 21st century. In order to maintain stability in the justice system, proper procedure must be followed. The code of ethics is a necessary tool in the criminal justice system, to protect the citizens of this country. In America's system the trial court is the big arena where justice is decided. Ethics are not to be taken lightly. At this stage of the system someone's fate will be determined. It is also where the best ethics should be practiced, although we have come to learn this is not always the case". I agree with what the books said because I am living with the consequences.

It's just a sad state of affairs. We have come to believe that the court system is the one place our rights will be protected, but I beg to differ.

All lawyers in the courtroom should be reaching out to the jurors showing them that good morals and good ethics are not just words, but a duty to our system. No antics, smoke screens, or bad ethics allowed.

Most people that receive these injustices are poor. This is a form of discrimination that is going unaddressed by wealthier America. As a moral obligation, Americans whether white, black, rich or poor should stand against discrimination in the system.

It is like cancer, it will eat away until it destroys the whole sum of the matter. In other words injustice will soon reach wealthy America too. The criminal justice system must be maintained with the code of ethics in each arena. This will give citizens the type of services intended by the founding fathers. No citizen's rights should ever be abused, including mine.

The future is good ethics, the more we help our justice system recognize the smallest hint of unethical behavior the less it will be experienced in generations to come. As more people stand behind those who have experienced unethical behavior, the more attention will be given to this disease that has attacked some of our citizens.

Good ethics will have a momentum that everyone will be thankful for. Although the criminal justice system revolves around the norms of society, it is far from producing its desired effects, which is to maintain social order, eliminate injustices and to give our communities a sense of peace.

When our judges and appellate courts see unethical behavior they should take action immediately, whether some lawyer was able to point it out in writing or not because sometimes the ethics are compromised by something as simple as case overload and we the people can end up paying with our lives.

I can speak this way because I've been victimized by this disease. I'm now on a mission called *Bad Ethics Prevention*, but I can't do it by myself. If anyone is against bad ethics, injustice, wrongful convictions, please help me by helping someone in your area suffering from this disease.

The rehearing was denied in June and Professor Watson was not surprised. She was not as sad as before and neither was I.

My questions remain, what the hell is going on with our system? Are we really the best in the world?

I can't tell anymore after my experience. Why would our system take a good guy and destroy his life and confidence in justice? I've done everything I could to live according to the laws of our land and this is my reward. As a citizen, my county and state has treated me like crap. No one in our government who was contacted would listen to me or respond to my concerns. So who do we call if our government won't listen to the voice of the people?

I wonder if this is the kind of treatment that sends some people over the edge. I always wondered how people could turn against their own kind. Is this why some with weaker minds than others become members of violent anti—government groups?

I am a true-blue American who was working on his American dream until it was abruptly cut off at the age of 31. What am I supposed to think of my beloved America?

I am hopeful, I won't give up and I pray that we all learn something from my experience that propels us to better not only our own lives but the lives of others as well because everybody is somebody and deserves to be treated as such know matter what color, sex, or economic status.

Most people believe I'm crazy for continuing to talk as though my blessings are about to come after sixteen years of disappointment from our legal system. But my faith and positive belief system is how I maintained my hope through years of being unjustly imprisoned. If you have no hope, you have no future.

There is a verse in the bible that says to call those things that be not as though they were. So I continue to see myself victorious even when I've only seen defeat because it's not over until it's over. I'm ready for the next round because I will fight as long as I can breathe and everyone involved knows that about me.

Whenever you are standing on the truth you know your fight is never over until you succeed. Because all your life you've been taught to believe that the truth shall set you free, and so you hold on to that truth like nothing else matters. Even when it seems to look impossible for that truth to come forth, you hold on to it that much tighter. When you know in your heart, mind, and soul that you're standing on the truth it gives you that extra confidence you need when all the doors seem to be closing on you. Don't let it break your spirit or steal your joy, because you're standing on what God loves "The Truth".

The Innocence NETWORK

In July 2009, I called the professor's office and she had so much excitement in her voice. I'm sure she still isn't aware of the positive energy she sent through the telephone that day. She explained that The Innocent Network had signed on to help fight against this wrongful conviction after reading Indiana's Court of Appeals decision to deny me a new fair trial.

She was inspired because years ago she had invited them to get involved in the appeals process but they declined. Since then a number of scientists have come forth and criticized Indiana's laboratory trial testimony. But they also understood that all updated DNA testing excluded all the suspects, including me, in this case.

This was great news because in addition to my team, legal minds all over the country would now support my fight for justice. They immediately filed a 12-page brief to support the professor's motion to transfer this case to the Indiana Supreme Court asking them to review the case as well.

The Network also stated why they had taken interest in the case. They are known by the court and other legal minds as *The Amicus Curiae*, a Latin word that basically means friend of the court who volunteers to offer information on a point of law. The Innocence Network is an association of organizations dedicated to providing pro bono legal and investigative services to prisoners for whom evidence discovered post-conviction can provide conclusive proof on innocence. The fifty-two current members of The Network represent hundreds of prisoners with innocence claims in all fifty states and the District of Columbia, as well as Australia, Canada, the United Kingdom, and New Zealand.

The Network and its members are also dedicated to improving the accuracy and reliability of the criminal justice system in future cases. Drawing on the lessons from cases in which innocent persons were convicted, The Network advocates study and reform designed to enhance the truth seeking functions of the criminal justice system to ensure that future wrongful convictions are prevented.

The Network pioneered the post-conviction DNA model that has to date exonerated 240 innocent people and has served as counsel in a majority of these cases. As perhaps the nation's leading authority on wrongful convictions, The Network and two of its founders, Barry Scheck and Peter Neufeld are regularly consulted by officials at the state, local and federal levels.

In over half of the 240 exonerations by the Innocence Network, the misapplication of forensic disciplines – such as blood type testing, hair analysis, finger print analysis, bite mark analysis, and more has played a role in convicting the innocent.

In these cases, forensic criminalist presented erroneous evidence to the judge or jury, which led to the wrongful conviction. This work has given Amicus a particularly strong interest in ensuring that criminal convictions are premised upon accurate forensic work.

The Innocence Network seeks to present a broad perspective on the issues in the hope that the risk of future wrongful convictions will be minimized.

The summary of their argument was that *this case presents the question as to the appropriate standard to apply in evaluating new exculpatory DNA evidence in post-conviction review under the Indiana DNA statute. Indiana was at the forefront in recognizing the seismic impact that advances in DNA testing and evidence have had on criminal convictions based on now outdated* and inaccurate science, and in 2001, Indiana enacted the DNA statue as a special remedial statute. Whereas here, DNA testing now exculpates an accused from an inference the state sought to establish by scientific evidence, a court must begin the remedial process by candidly acknowledging the "stark reality" as recently stated by the Kentucky Supreme Court that a person was convicted with evidence now known to be fundamentally false. That conclusion does not involve bad intent or bad conduct. Rather, it only involves the validity of the science.

To prove a crucial issue at Glenn's 1993 trial that he was present at the vicious attack, the state presented serology evidence that Glenn could not be excluded from a semen sample and that his hair matched a hair sample found on the victim's sweater on all twenty-six characteristics that were tested. Improved DNA testing also provided exculpatory evidence that the semen and hair were conclusively not from Glenn.

The state conceded that its serology and hair evidence would not be admissible against Glenn in a trial today. In analyzing whether Glenn was entitled to a new trial, the PCR court both applied the wrong standard of review and failed to properly consider the impact of the newly exculpatory DNA evidence. Ignoring the remedial purpose of the statue and the

123

stark reality of this case that fundamentally false evidence was used against Glenn. The PCR court denied relief because the DNA evidence did not exonerate him, then, the PCR court looked at the remaining non-scientific evidence against him without considering the totality of the evidence that a jury would hear today – devoid of the scientific serology and hair evidence that the state had presented at trial.

The court of Appeals failed to correct these errors. Instead a PCR court should apply the standard set forth in Indiana's remedial DNA statue that grants a new trial where new DNA evidence is favorable to a petitioner, and where there is a reasonable probability that a petitioner would not have been convicted with the benefit of the new DNA evidence. Furthermore, in considering the newly exculpatory evidence, a PCR court should consider the impact that scientific evidence, or the lack there of, would have had on the jury's consideration of any other evidence. This case is the ideal vehicle to correct this erroneous determination and to set forth the appropriate test for granting a new trial under Indiana's remedial DNA statute. No preliminary issue is presented. The post-conviction testing has occurred. The results are not disputed; the state conceded that serology and hair comparison evidence is no longer used, having been trumped by more accurate forms of DNA testing. Thus, this court should utilize this case as a means to set forth the proper standard for Indiana courts to apply when considering newly exculpatory DNA evidence and, because Glenn meets that standard, grant him a new trial.

Amicus went on to argue three main points over approximately 10 pages. The first point was the fact that the state's exculpatory scientific evidence at trial would be inadmissible today. Second point, the PCR court misapplied the Indiana Code Standard. Third point, the PCR court failed to properly weigh the newly exculpatory evidence. Amicus concluded these arguments by stating that the Indiana DNA Statue affirms a petitioner's statutory right to a new trial once he demonstrates a reasonable probability – not a certainty – which a jury considering the evidence as it stands today would fail to convict him. Glenn has amply surmounted that barrier. Glenn seeks the opportunity for a new, fair trial where the remaining evidence against him must stand alone, without false corroboration by discredited science. The PCR court misapplied the standard and improperly weighed the evidence. Thus, this court should set forth the proper standard and grant Glenn a new trial.

The arguments of Amicus (The Network) to the Indiana Supreme Court were just the sweetest sounds to my ears. These three arguments where enhanced by the questions and arguments presented on transfer by Professor Watson. Combined, I thought this would be devastating for the state and almost impossible to overcome. You notice I used the words almost impossible because in law there are no guarantees, as you can see by my fight thus far. But nevertheless, I couldn't be more thrilled, knowing that on July 24, 2009 Professor Watson's Wrongful Conviction Program with the support of The Innocence Network filed petitions for transfer to Indiana's highest court on my behalf.

In my mind's eye this day was the sight and effect of the ultimate power of prayer. No one could possibly understand the celebration my heart was experiencing on the inside. I know I hadn't received the decision I had long waited for, but as I said before seeing prayers come to pass was victory in and of itself regardless of what the court or man might do or say.

I know it's now all about more of the waiting game. This is what most people would say or think, but I differ because my wait is only upon God above. So I keep moving forward knowing that my blessing is on the way know matter what!

You see, I continue to search for my continued peace and understanding in all things. I also realize that I do live in this present world conditions along with my family and loved ones in which we may all suffer from some heartache and pain by the unwanted decisions in this world, today that's reality. "Oh my God, after 16 years of heartache and tears, constant fight, perseverance, most of all the truth. As of October 2, 2009 the Indiana Supreme Court has not removed the smoke screen, the confusion, the distortion, and the shackles acts of deceit. They have agreed to keep this conviction against me as the lower courts suggested.

Damn it! Hold on, let me keep my head held high because I know in this game played with my life someone would win and someone would lose. The hope is for the innocent to always win, but that is not always the case as shown here. This fight is not over. I will continue my mission of clearing my name after my release from prison. It can no longer be a fight for justice since I have completed the time for this crime. The fight now can only be to restore my good name. My next step will be to ask the Federal Court System to review this case. I know this request is also based on my hope and faith. My release from prison is in 50 days and what a day of rejoicing that will be. I will continue my journey strong in hope, faith, and joy this is the gift God has blessed me with and no one can take it away.

<u>Glenn's Law</u>

What I want is for our legislators to mandate the DNA statute to:

A) Overcome circumstantial evidence (disputed points of facts) when the new testing exculpates a defendant seeking a new trial under newly discovered evidence or whatever relief is proper,

B) Automatically reverse a case for new trial when new evidence shows old evidence was false - unless direct evidence points to guilt, and

C) Cannot be cured with a procedural default of any sort. This law should be called *Favorable Exculpation Rule.*

<u>My Conclusion</u>

As far as our justice system it's going to take all of us to come together to lower the rate of wrongful convictions. It's not enough for just a few to get out of prison who are innocent, and say "too bad" about everyone who is left behind. It shouldn't work that way. We are all apart of each other because we're all a part of the human race. We can all grow up and be mature men and women to come against injustices, with the unity of faith we can overcome this new disease that's separating our families. Do you know what it feels like watching your children grow up hurting because their father is not there for them or watching your children grow up mad at you, but when they become old enough to understand they begin to try to turn that anger and confusion into love and respect for you. Now they're trying to love you because you're their dad at least that's the title they put with your name because year after year you grow apart. No matter how hard you try to make your relationships work with your children, no matter how many visits you have with your children week after week year after year it becomes apparent that you really don't even know each other.

The separation has caused too much damage. So now the most important people in your life that you love more than anything in this world, don't even know each other.

Even though I'm being freed on November 24, 2009 regardless of what happens in the court system my nightmare is not over. Now I'm going to a place that I'm unfamiliar with not knowing what to expect but I'm blessed because my family and children are going to do their best to help me through this nightmare until it's over, if it can ever be over.

I lost in this game that was played by the system and when I lost my pain spilled over into all my family and loved ones. Now, being a victim of this game called justice the number of victims didn't stop at me, but also those who love me have become victims of injustice. How do we stop the pain of this nightmare? Is there a cure? How do we get back the years of a man's' life? Do we have to wait for every family to experience the pain and suffering of an injustice before the proper steps are put in place to prevent wrongful convictions, injustices, "Innocent Nightmares", is what I call it.

I beg the people of our country to get out and support organizations such as Professor Watson's Wrongful Conviction Program and The Innocence Network. These people are trying to save American lives and American families. The Bible tells us to destroy a person's reputation takes from that person a most precious gift, his good name. A good name is more desirable than great riches. Rebuilding my name starts November 24, 2009 and I hope this is the day my sadness, my cries, my pain comes to a permanent end, with this day starting a new beginning of happiness for my family and me.

And to the victim I must say: You too, were denied justice. Because two innocent men were convicted of the travesty that happened to you – those who are guilty remained free. You were left to wonder if justice had been served. You had to relive what happened every time an appeal was raised. And for that I truly apologize. I know that some people have not believed in my innocence, but right now all that matters is the fact that my family and friends believe in my innocence and now I'm being freed completing the sentence of 36 years with 18 to do. Many lawyers and legal minds know of my innocence and now maybe even you know, understand and agree. As I continue my fight to clear my name, I ask that you would pray for me and my family.

I want to thank Professor Fran Watson for taking on this very complex case and all the students of Indiana University Law Clinics who worked countless hours alongside her.

These men and women restored my confidence in believing that good morals, and good ethics do still exist in our system even though I've experienced a travesty of justice. People like this should be rewarded for the professionalism and for extending a helping hand to American citizens who are in need of their help I *had fainted, unless I had believed to see the goodness of the Lord in the land of the living.* PS 27:13. Thank you all with my most sincere gratitude.

My case to date

On August 15, 2014, I received the news of a new DNA test by Cyber Genetics called True Allele. This test is becoming more accepted by many states and its use is growing across the country (mostly used by prosecutors). This test is able to identify small amounts of DNA left at crime scenes and also able to identify mixtures of DNA.

On August 8, 2014 this test was applied to the evidence in my case.

True Allele was able to identify five perpetrators which confirms the victim's statement of five attackers who assaulted her, but the problem for the state is that Glenn is excluded as well as co-defendants and all other suspects in this case, which confirms that we did not commit the crime and a rush to judgment by the detective and prosecutors is now brought to light. The necessary legal papers are being filed on behalf of myself and my co-defendant with the hopes of clearing our names.

My goal is to be exonerated from all charges against me and to receive retribution for the years that I was unjustly imprisoned. In the mean-time I'm allowing God to work all these things together for my good. If things don't work out the way I desire, I'm just believing that they are working out according to God's plan for me which is more important than man's plan.

Although I was a good man when I was imprisoned, I was not a man of faith. Prison revealed to me the course of faith I needed to live by and revealed the man God always intended for me to become. Prison did not kill me, it birthed God's power in me.

And as a man of faith, I know that what was meant for evil, God is using for good for me, my family and my community.

In the end, it really is about what God wants to do with my circumstances and it matters not what man thinks. God is sovereign, He is in control and I trust him with my trials and with my life. My responsibility is to live my life, flaws and all, in a way that glorifies God and does not glorify the unfairness of life.

I seek to make others better, to make the system better and prayerfully my story shows those in power where they need to change and helps those negatively affected by those in power to see a way to overcome, endure, persevere and be the better man.

*I know that you are **pleased** with me,*
for my enemy does not triumph over me.
*Because of my **integrity** you uphold me and*
*set me **in your presence forever**.*
Psalm 41:11-12 NIV

2014 - Deacon Ordination

Deacon Ordination with mom and the Pastor in Gary, Indiana

REFERENCES

Schmalleger, Frank. *Criminal Justice Today: An Introductory Text for the 21st Century* (10th Edition), Prentice Hall; 10 Edition, 2008, Print.

Trent, Mary Alice. *Ethics in the 21st Century*, Longman; 1 edition, 2004, Print.

Contact me at:

innocentnightmareglenn@gmail.com

Made in the USA
Middletown, DE
23 March 2022

63108345R00080